Advanced Introduction to Corporate Finance

Advanced Introduction to

Corporate Finance

JAMES A. BRICKLEY
Simon Business School, University of Rochester, USA

CLIFFORD W. SMITH JR.
Simon Business School, University of Rochester, USA

Elgar Advanced Introductions

 Edward Elgar
PUBLISHING

Cheltenham, UK • Northampton, MA, USA

Published by
Edward Elgar Publishing Limited
The Lypiatts
15 Lansdown Road
Cheltenham
Glos GL50 2JA
UK

Edward Elgar Publishing, Inc.
William Pratt House
9 Dewey Court
Northampton
Massachusetts 01060
USA

A catalogue record for this book
is available from the British Library

Library of Congress Control Number: 2022931168

Printed on elemental chlorine free (ECF)
recycled paper containing 30% Post-Consumer Waste

ISBN 978 1 80220 097 3 (cased)
ISBN 978 1 80220 098 0 (eBook)
ISBN 978 1 80220 099 7 (paperback)

Printed and bound in the USA

Contents

Figures

Tables

Preface

Managers in all corporations must decide in which projects to invest; how they should be financed; what to pay to shareholders; and in what form. Finance and economic scholars have devoted significant effort over the past 60-plus years to develop theoretical insights and related evidence to help guide managers in these managerially important decisions. The purpose of this book is to provide an advanced introduction to the modern theory of corporate finance and to summarize the related empirical evidence. In our analysis we continually stress managerial insights and implications.

The target audience for this book is quite broad. Of course, managers responsible for aspects of the finance function should find this a useful review and update, even if they have an MBA but graduated several years ago. And with the increased use of cross-functional business teams (including members with individual expertise in strategy, product design, manufacturing, finance, accounting, human resource management, marketing, sales, etc.), it is important for managers across these specialties to have a broad understanding of each of these functional areas. This book should provide this basic understanding in finance. It can be used as a text on a short course on corporate finance or within a more general business survey course or as an introductory or supplemental text on a longer corporate finance course. Business students might find it a useful pre-read prior to taking a longer and more detailed course on the subject. Corporate finance instructors may find the book helpful in suggesting how to organize the material in their courses and in providing useful examples for class.

Much of the theoretical work in finance has become quite mathematical; moreover, the empirical methods used in testing the theory have employed increasingly sophisticated statistical techniques. We, however, have written this book so that readers without strong backgrounds in either mathematics or statistics can understand the key concepts and managerial insights. Throughout the book, we stress the intuition behind the key results and illustrate them through simple, understandable examples, rather than through complex mathematical proofs. We provide a detailed set of references for those readers who want to delve more deeply into any given topic.

The book is organized as follows. In Chapter 1 we provide a historical overview of the field and present five basic building blocks in financial economics that we use in subsequent chapters. Our focus in Chapter 2 is on capital budgeting – how managers should evaluate and decide which of the firm's investment opportunities to pursue. We present the theory, evidence, and managerial insights related to the firm's financing decision in Chapters 3 through 7 – what mix of debt and equity to use in financing the firm's operations and investments. In Chapter 8 we focus on corporate payout policy – the amount and form of distributions to shareholders. We present a condensed summary of key managerial insights and our concluding remarks in Chapter 9.

1 The theory of corporate finance: historical overview and basic building blocks[1]

1.1   Introduction

Corporate finance is broadly concerned with three major decisions: (1) choosing projects in which to invest – *capital budgeting*, (2) choosing how to finance the firm's investments and operations – *capital structure/ financing policy*, and (3) choosing how much and in what form (dividends or share repurchases) to distribute funds to the firm's shareholders – *payout policy*. Prior to the middle of the 20th century, finance literature provided little systematic guidance for managers on any of these decisions. Rather, this literature consisted of a great deal of institutional detail, plus rules of thumb and *ad hoc* "theories." Beginning in the late 1950s and early 1960s, the analytic methods and techniques traditional to economics began to be applied to problems in finance.

This evolution was accompanied by a change in focus from normative questions such as *What should investment, financing or dividend policies be?* to positive theories addressing questions such as *What are the effects of alternate investment, financing, or dividend policies on the value of the firm?* This shift in emphasis was necessary to provide the scientific basis for the formation and analysis of corporate policy decisions.

Financial executives understandably are focused on answering normative questions; providing these answers is at the very heart of their managerial responsibilities. But it is important to recognize that sound positive theories provide better answers to these normative questions – they provide decision makers a better understanding of the consequences of their choices. Purposeful decisions simply cannot be made without explicit (or at least implicit) use of positive theories. Managers cannot decide what action to take and expect to meet their objectives without some idea of how alternative actions might affect outcomes – and that is precisely what is meant by a positive theory (Jensen, 1983). For example, to choose among alternative financial structures, a manager wants to know how their various potential choices might affect expected net cash flows, the level of risk, and therefore firm value. Using incorrect positive theories leads to decisions that have unexpected (and frequently undesirable) consequences.

The years since the 1950s have produced a large body of theoretical and empirical work on corporate finance. While we still lack a comprehensive positive theory that covers all aspects of corporate finance, the field has made great progress. Many useful managerial insights can be drawn from what we now know. In this chapter, we summarize the historical development of five basic building blocks that comprise the foundation for the modern theory of financial economics. In subsequent chapters, we employ these building blocks to provide a more detailed analysis of the three primary corporate financial decisions – capital budgeting, capital structure/financing policy, and payout policy.

1.2   Fundamental building blocks

The years since 1950 have witnessed the formation of five major building blocks of the modern theory of financial economics. These are:

- Efficient Markets Theory
- Portfolio Theory
- Capital Asset Pricing Theory
- Option Pricing Theory
- Agency Theory

These theories have evolved over time in roughly this order. Below, we briefly summarize each with an emphasis on aspects central to corporate finance.

1.2.1   Efficient markets theory

The *Efficient Markets Hypothesis* holds that a market is efficient if it is impossible to make economic profits by trading on available information. Samuelson (1965) and Mandelbrot (1966) lay the foundation for the modern theoretical rationale underlying the Efficient Markets

Hypothesis. Samuelson reasons that if prices reflect available information, then price changes must reflect new information. But to qualify as "new" information, it must not be possible to be deduced from prior information. Therefore, almost by definition, "new" information must be uncorrelated over time, and hence, so must price changes.

The term *Efficient Capital Markets* has several related meanings. Despite the similarity in language, most of the efficient markets literature in finance has developed independently of the basic notions of economic efficiency from welfare economics. Yet Smith (1991) and Roll (1994) suggest a way to think about market efficiency that helps bridge this gap: *Consider a market to be efficient if the marginal investment in information yields a normal rate of return.* This definition permits a closer parallel with efficiency notions in economics. It also raises two important points.

First, notions about efficiency are driven ultimately by arbitrage arguments – the idea that if close substitutes sell for different prices, you should buy what is cheap and sell what is dear until the price difference is too small to cover transactions costs. Costs of engaging in arbitrage place limits on profitable trading, and thus transactions costs should be included in studies designed to examine potential market inefficiencies.

Second, the set of available information must be identified. *Weak-Form Efficiency* restricts a security's information set to its past price history. *Semi-Strong-Form Efficiency* considers the information set to be all publicly available information. *Strong-Form Efficiency* considers all information, both public and private.

Weak-Form Efficiency. Securities markets are Weak-Form Efficient if past prices and trends cannot be used to predict future price changes. Weak-Form Market Efficiency implies that stock prices follow a *random walk* – each successive price movement is an independent draw from a distribution. Early empirical analyses by statisticians such as Working (1934), Kendall (1953), and Osborne (1959, 1962) lay the foundation for this theory. These statisticians examine data from stock and commodity prices expecting to find recurring price cycles. To their (as well as others') surprise, their analyses identify no discernable cycles in the data. Their evidence implies that stock and commodity prices behave as a random walk – that is that security price changes behave as if they are independent random drawings.

This evidence also is instrumental in prompting Samuelson and Mandelbrot to provide the theoretical foundation for the Efficient Markets Hypothesis. Although stock prices can drift upward over time (if the mean of the price-change distribution is positive), price changes are uncorrelated with past price changes. *Technical Analysis*, which uses past price movements to forecast future prices, thus is unlikely to be productive.[2]

Semi-Strong-Form Efficiency. Within a Semi-Strong-Form Efficient Market, prices respond quickly to new publicly available information; it thus is impossible to earn systematic economic profits by trading on information after its public release. In examining this hypothesis, researchers have studied stock price reactions to a broad array of different announcements – for example, earnings releases, takeover announcements, dividend announcements, and announcements of new security offerings. In general, the evidence provides quite consistent support for this hypothesis: Markets appear to respond to new information quickly, and it is difficult – if not impossible – to make systematic abnormal returns by trading on information after its public release. Moreover, mutual fund managers of active funds tend to underperform the market after expenses.[3] And mutual funds that are top performers in one period generally have no more than an average chance of being a top performer in subsequent periods. This evidence has led many investors to invest in low-cost index funds, such as Vanguard's S&P 500 Index Fund, that simply try to track the stock market, which on average has increased over time.

Perhaps the strongest evidence for market efficiency comes from former President of the American Finance Association, Richard Roll (1994): "After spending 25 years looking at particular allegations of market inefficiencies, and 10 years attempting to exploit them as a practicing money manager, by actually trading significant amounts of money according to trading rules suggested by the 'inefficiencies' … I have never yet found one that worked in practice."

The Semi-Strong-Form of market efficiency implies that *Fundamental Analysis*, which attempts to measure the intrinsic value of a security by analyzing economic and financial information – including the company's financial statements and other publicly available information – will not produce systematically positive economic returns. And even though some evidence appears inconsistent with the Semi-Strong-Form Efficiency Hypothesis, in most circumstances both managers and investors should assume that securities markets are Semi-Strong-Form Efficient (at least within developed markets).

Strong-Form Efficiency. Securities markets are Strong-Form Efficient if it is impossible to make economic profits from trading either on publicly available or on inside information. Securities markets are unlikely to be Strong-Form Efficient (this hypothesis is included because it lies at the end of this spectrum of logical possibilities). It is safe to assume that managers often have private information, which is yet to be revealed to the public that when announced would likely affect firm value, such as quarterly earnings and takeover offers before they are announced to the public. The most compelling evidence for an informational disparity between managers and investors is from studies of insider trading. When corporate executives trade in their own company's stock, they systematically out-perform market averages. This evidence shows that managers have access to more information than is reflected in current stock prices – that is, these executives are inframarginal. An investor with access to such non-public information presumably could make abnormal returns by trading on the information if they were not precluded from doing so by insider-trading laws. If capital markets were completely (Strong-Form) efficient, then the market value of the firm would reflect the present value of the firm's expected future net cash flows – including cash flows from unannounced future investment opportunities. One person quipped: "Being a CEO would be a lot easier if markets were Strong-Form Efficient: I could just think of taking a project and proceed if the stock price goes up and discard the project if it goes down."

Informational Asymmetries. We doubt that the corporate finance implications of this information disparity between managers and investors are as straightforward as some would suggest. Investors know managers often possess superior information. But there is an important difference between insider trades and other transactions that might exploit their informational advantage. Insider trades are announced only after the trade occurs. However, if managers undertake observable actions that might allow them to exploit their informational advantage, investors are "put on notice" and market prices should adjust. Moreover, a reputation for exploiting informational advantages at investors' expense is a liability – one that reduces managers' incentives to extract short-run gains.

For example, suppose that the market price of a stock is $25.00. Investors understand that its real value, if they had access to the same information as the firm's managers, might be as high as $27.00 or as low as $23.00. But given the investors' current information, $25.00 is a fair price. Now let's suppose corporate managers announce that the firm is selling new shares. They might reason that were managers assessment of value $27.00, selling shares at a price of $25.00 would be selling shares at a price below their true value – an opportunity cost for the firm. But if their assessment of value were $23.00, and they could sell these new shares at $25.00, then the firm would be accessing "cheap" money. Such reasoning would lead investors to reassess their own assessments of value – the likelihood of the shares being worth $27.00 is reduced, of being $23.00 is increased, and thus the current price of $25.00 is too high. As a result, the current market price of the shares falls. This basic logic plays an important role in some of the theoretical discussions of firm financing policies presented later in this book.

Managerial Implications. In summary, there is some debate about the degree to which markets are Semi-Strong-Form Efficient and whether securities are always rationally priced. Nonetheless, the extent to which financial markets fall short of the ideal of Strong-Form Efficiency still places an upper bound on certain concerns. It should be noted that the Efficient Markets Hypothesis is perhaps the most tested hypothesis in all the social sciences, and the existing evidence strongly suggests that securities markets are quite efficient. Based on this evidence, managers generally should assume that stocks and bonds are appropriately priced and that there are few profits to be made by trading on publicly available information. This perspective yields several important managerial implications:

1. Securities markets are forward looking. If the firm announces it is undertaking a costly investment that is expected to increase the firm's future net cash flows, the present value of these expected flows will be quickly and accurately incorporated into the current stock price. Market prices thus can provide important feedback to managers about the future. For example, if managers were to announce a prospective merger that causes their firm's stock price to drop significantly, they should think carefully before proceeding with the transaction.
2. Managers should maximize the current market value of the firm (subject to existing laws and regulations). Moreover, there is no ambi-

guity about the firm's objective function – specifically, management does not have to choose between maximizing the firm's current value or its future value.

3. There is little benefit to manipulating earnings per share. Management decisions that increase earnings, but do not affect cash flows, represent wasted effort. Managerial bonus plans, earnings-based debt covenants, and other factors might motivate managers to "manage earnings." However, it is unlikely that the market will be fooled by earnings manipulations for long, and earnings management potentially violates securities laws and regulations.

4. In an efficient market, new securities are issued at market prices that reflect an unbiased assessment of their future payoffs. Accordingly, concerns about dilution or the sharing of positive net present value projects with new security holders are eliminated, or at least significantly reduced. Managers also should not waste their time trying to forecast upswings and downswings in their firm's stock price based on past price trends or other publicly available information.

5. Managers generally should trust market prices. Managers in charge of their firm's securities portfolio, exchange-rate policy, and so on should avoid speculative positions based on their personal forecasts of security prices, interest rates, or exchange rates. Managers are unlikely to beat the market if they engage in speculative trading, and such trading can impose significant risks on the firm.

6. Security returns provide meaningful measures of firm and managerial performance. Stock-based managerial compensation plans are logically and prominently used in many publicly traded companies to provide incentives to senior executives. Securities regulators, in turn, require publicly traded firms to compare their companies' stock returns with relevant peer groups in their annual proxy statements.

1.2.2   Portfolio theory

Most investors are *risk averse*: For a given expected rate of return, they prefer lower return volatility (as measured by variance or standard deviation). It has long been recognized that return variability can be reduced through diversification. For example, by holding a portfolio consisting of umbrella company and suntan lotion company shares, exposure to the vagaries of weather is reduced. Exposure to other types of risks can be reduced by including other investments in the portfolio. As noted by the famous mathematician Daniel Bernoulli in 1738: "it is advisable to divide goods which are exposed to some small danger into several portions rather than to risk them all together." Or, as the old adage advises, "don't put all your eggs in one basket."[4] Finally, this basic idea underlies the entire insurance industry: Although the risk associated with an individual life insurance policy might be great, and even though the company is unable to predict the death of any of its individual policyholders, by putting a large number of similar policies together, total claims become quite predictable.

Prior to the middle of the 20th century, despite the accumulation of all of this theory and practical experience, within financial markets, scant attention is given to portfolio composition. Security analysts focus primarily on picking undervalued securities and identifying overvalued securities. Investors' portfolios simply would be the accumulated result of their attempts to buy securities at low prices and to sell them at high prices.

Nobel laureate Harry Markowitz changes all of this when he publishes his pathbreaking analysis of portfolio selection in 1952. Markowitz demonstrates that it is not a security's total risk (as measured by its return variance) that is important to investors, but the contribution of the security to the riskiness of the entire portfolio. This contribution depends on how the returns on the security covary with the returns on the other securities within the portfolio. Markowitz recognizes that while diversification reduces risk, it generally will not eliminate it; security returns tend to be positively correlated (for example, most are exposed to common macroeconomic factors, such as swings in the economy and inflation).

Markowitz defines the efficient set of portfolios as those that maximize expected return for a given variance and minimize variance for a given expected return. Figure 1.1 illustrates an efficient investment "frontier." Portfolios located on the frontier are efficient in the sense that it is not possible to increase the expected return by investing in another portfolio without increasing variance or to reduce the variance without lowering the expected return. Portfolios located inside the efficient frontier are inefficient since by investing in an efficient portfolio, it is possible to increase the expected return without increasing risk and/or reduce risk without reducing expected return.

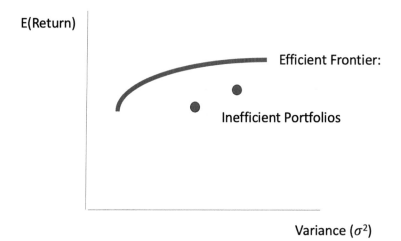

Figure 1.1   Efficient investment frontier

Portfolios located on the frontier are efficient: expected return cannot be increased by investing in another portfolio without increasing the variance or to reduce the variance without lowering the expected return. Portfolios located inside the efficient frontier are inefficient.

Managerial Implications. Modern portfolio theory has important implications for corporate finance professionals. Firms generally will not lower their cost of capital if they reduce the variance of their earnings through corporate diversification. Investors can achieve this same reduction in risk in their personal portfolios, typically at lower cost. Firms sometimes can lower expected bankruptcy costs through actions that reduce their earnings volatility (thus affecting cash flows and value). But this often can be achieved less expensively through derivative contracts in financial markets than through corporate diversification. If corporate diversification is to increase firm value, there generally must be synergies (that is economies of scale or scope) that increase the net cash flows of the combined operations.

1.2.3   Capital asset pricing theory

Markowitz's analysis is primarily *normative* in nature – how investors *should* select their portfolios. In the 1960s, Nobel laureate Bill Sharpe, as well as Lintner and Treynor, extended Markowitz's analysis to create a *positive* theory of the determination of asset prices. Given investor demands for securities implied by Markowitz's mean-variance framework, these economists derive equilibrium security prices within a single-period setting, assuming a fixed supply of assets, with no taxes, and the ability of investors to lend or borrow at the risk-free rate.

Although total risk is measured by the variance of portfolio returns, these models imply that in equilibrium an individual security is priced to reflect its contribution to total risk (or its "systematic risk"), measured by the covariance of its return with the return on the market portfolio of all assets. The simplest form of the Capital Asset Pricing Model (CAPM) yields the following expression for the equilibrium expected return, $E(R_j)$, on asset j:

$$E(R_j) = r + \beta_j \left[E(R_M) - r \right]$$

(1.1)

where r is the riskless rate of interest, $E(R_M)$ is the expected rate of return on the market portfolio of all assets; and $\beta_j = \text{cov}(R_j, R_M) / \text{var}(R_M)$ is the covariance between the return on asset j and the market return divided by the variance of the market return. β_j ("beta") is the measure of the systematic risk of security j – that risk which is priced by the market. The beta of a stock can be estimated relatively easily through regression analysis – virtually all major financial services companies publish estimated betas for publicly traded companies. Figure 1.2 displays *Security Market Line*, which depicts how the expected return on a security depends on its beta.

All economic models are simplified representations of reality. There have been many tests of the CAPM, and not surprisingly this simple model fails to explain perfectly the pricing of securities in actual markets. Alternatives, such as the Arbitrage Pricing Model, Black's Two-Factor Model, and the Fama-French Multifactor Model, have subsequently been developed. None of these alternatives is perfect either.

Managerial Implications. Today's financial professionals vary in their preferred model (all have costs and benefits). For example, the CAPM is still commonly used, but some prefer to use a multi-factor model. The use of asset pricing models benefits corporate managers by allowing them to define the opportunity cost of capital for their firms' capital budgeting decisions. The required rate of return on a company's stock is not observable, and these models provide a mechanism for estimating it. Ultimately a firm should only invest in a project if the project's expected return is greater than the project's cost of capital (as we discuss in more detail in Chapter 2).

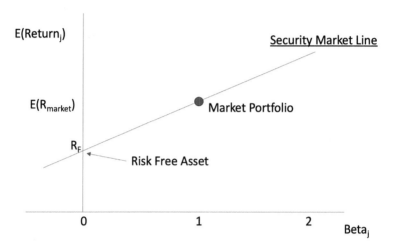

Figure 1.2   Security Market Line

The Capital Asset Pricing Model (CAPM) predicts that the expected return on a security will be a linear function of its beta, which is a measure of the security's contribution to the risk of the overall market portfolio, i.e., its "systematic risk." The equation for the Security Market Line is E(Rj) = RF + [E(RM) – RF]Bj, where Bj = cov(Rj, RM)/var (RM).

All asset pricing models produce two important implications for financial managers and investors (Brealey, Myers and Allen, 2020): (1) Investors demand a higher expected rate of return to accept more risk; (2) The relevant risk of an individual security, the risk that is priced in the market, depends primarily on its systematic risk – the risk that cannot be managed effectively by simply including it in a well-diversified portfolio.

1.2.4   Option pricing theory

Following the publication of the Black-Scholes (1973) paper in which the pricing models for simple put and call options are derived originally, there has been much work employing the continuous-time option-pricing analysis which they pioneered. We next summarize these developments, which represent a fundamental advancement in the theory of finance.[5]

Perhaps the simplest option is a European call – an option to buy a stipulated asset on the maturity date of the contract for a stated price. Fischer Black and his co-author Nobel laureate Myron Scholes demonstrate that a riskless hedge can be created using the proper proportions of call options and shares of the underlying stock. Since the hedge is instantaneously riskless, as long as perfect substitutes are priced to yield the same rate of return, then the rate of return to the hedge will equal the riskless rate. From this equilibrium condition the call price can be obtained. Their solution to the European call pricing problem is:

$$c = SN\left\{\frac{\ln\left(\frac{S}{X}\right)+\left(r+\frac{\sigma^2}{2}\right)T}{\sigma\sqrt{T}}\right\} - e^{-rT}XN\left\{\frac{\ln\left(\frac{S}{X}\right)+\left(r-\frac{\sigma^2}{2}\right)T}{\sigma\sqrt{T}}\right\}$$

(1.2)

where c is the call price, S is the stock price, X is the option's exercise price, T is the option's time to maturity, σ^2 is the stock's variance rate, r is the risk-free interest rate, and N{z} is the cumulative standard normal distribution from minus infinity to z. Figure 1.3 illustrates the relation between the call price and the stock price, holding the exercise price, the time to maturity, the variance rate, and the riskless rate fixed. Academics found it surprising that their solution depends on just five variables, given the prior unsuccessful efforts to value options. The solution can be written in general form as:

$$c = c(S, X, T, \sigma^2, r)$$

(1.3)

where

$$\frac{\partial c}{\partial S} > 0; \frac{\partial c}{\partial X} < 0; \frac{\partial c}{\partial T} > 0; \frac{\partial c}{\partial \sigma^2} > 0; \frac{\partial c}{\partial r} > 0$$

These partial effects have intuitive interpretations: As the stock price increases, the expected payoff of the option increases. With a higher exercise price, more must be paid to exercise the option, and thus the expected payoff decreases. With a longer time to maturity or with a higher interest rate, the present value of the exercise price is lower, thus increasing the value of the option.[6] Finally, with a longer time to maturity or with a higher variance rate of the underlying stock price, the probability of a large price change in the security during the life of the option is greater. Since the call price cannot be negative, a larger range of possible stock prices increases the maximum value of the option without lowering its minimum value.

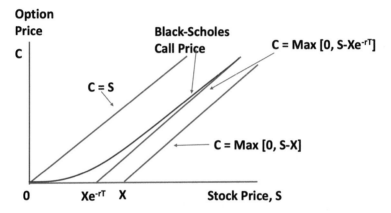

Figure 1.3   Black-Scholes call option price

This diagram displays the Black-Scholes call option price for different stock prices, with a given interest rate, variance rate, and time to maturity. The Black-Scholes call option price lies below the maximum possible value, $C = S$ (except where $S = 0$) and above the minimum value, $C = \text{Max} [0, S - Xe^{-rt}]$. Note that the curve relating the Black-Scholes call price with the stock price asymptotically approaches $C = \text{Max} [0, S - Xe^{-rt}]$ line.
Source: Variations of this basic figure are found throughout the literature on option pricing. This is based on Figure 1 in Smith (1976) and Figure 4.1 in Smith (1979).

Managerial Implications. This model for pricing options (and its various extensions) is widely used by option traders and numerous finance professionals. Black and Scholes also note that this option pricing analysis can be used to value other contingent claims, such as the equity of a simple levered firm. In this view, the equity of a leveraged firm is like a call option on the total value of the firm's assets with an exercise price equal to the face value of the firm's (zero coupon) bonds and an expiration date equal to the maturity date of the debt. Their analysis shows that the value of the firm's equity is an increasing function of the value of the firm's assets, the time to maturity of the firm's debt, the variance rate of the firm's assets, the risk-free rate, and a decreasing function of the face value of the firm's debt.

Many important corporate policy problems require the valuation of assets which, like call options or the equity value of simple levered firms, have payoffs that are contingent on the future value of another asset. Examples include options managers have in the timing of investment projects, options to expand successful projects, and options to abandon unsuccessful ones; moreover, managers can employ options to hedge risk exposures.

1.2.5 Agency theory[7]

Incentive Conflicts within Firms. It is useful to think of a firm as the *focal point of a set of contracts*. This definition focuses on the fact that the firm ultimately is a creation of the legal system that grants it the legal standing of an individual in a court of law. For example, Apple Inc. can enter contracts, sue, be sued, and so on. The term focal point indicates that the firm always is one of the parties to each of the many contracts that comprise the firm (some of which are only implicit). Examples of these contracts are stocks, bonds, loans, employee contracts, supplier contracts, customer warranties, leases, franchise agreements, and insurance contracts (see Figure 1.4)

Economic theory characterizes individuals as creative maximizers of their *own utility*. Thus, the collection of individuals that contract with the firm are unlikely to have objectives that are automatically aligned. For example, shareholders will generally want to maximize the price of the firm's common stock, even if doing so increases the risk borne by the firm's bondholders substantially. In contrast, bondholders will want the firm to take actions that limit the likelihood that the firm might default on their promised payments. Managers, in turn, potentially are more interested in their own compensation and perquisites (for example, exclusive club memberships, lavish office furniture, and corporate airplanes) than in maximizing firm value.

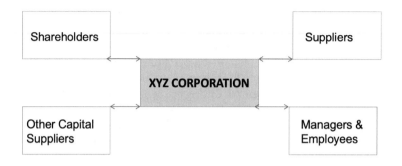

Figure 1.4   The firm as a focal point of contracts

A firm can be thought of as a focal point of contracts. The firm, which has the legal standing of an individual, is always one of the parties to all contracts that comprise the firm. This simplified figure illustrates some of the key contracting parties observed in most firms.

Agency Problems and their Costs. Jensen and Meckling define an *agency relationship* as a contract in which one or more persons [the principal(s)] engage another person [the agent] to perform some service on their behalf, which requires the delegation of some decision-making authority. A simple example is the owner of a firm hiring a manager to run it. Here the *agency problem* is that the manager can have incentives to take actions for personal benefit that harm the owner.

Asymmetric information and contracting costs typically preclude costless resolution of agency problems. Since the principal cannot observe the actions of the agent costlessly, the agent generally can engage in activities, such as shirking and excessive perquisite consumption, without those activities invariably being detected by the principal. Nonetheless, the principal usually can limit such behavior by establishing appropriate incentives for the agent through the structure of the contract and by incurring *monitoring costs*. Also, agents might incur *bonding costs* to help guarantee that they will not take certain actions or to ensure that the principal will be compensated if they do (for example, agents might bond themselves by purchasing insurance policies that pay the principal in the case of theft). Agents are willing to incur these expenses to increase the amount principals pay for the agents' services.

Since it is costly to control agency problems, it generally will not pay for either party to incur sufficient costs to ensure that the agent will follow the wishes of the principal completely – at some point the incremental cost of negotiating, administering, and enforcing the contract exceeds any additional benefits of additional expenditures to increase compliance. Jensen and Meckling define the dollar equivalent of the loss in the gains from trade that results from this divergence of interests within the agency relationship as the *residual loss*. This opportunity cost can be quite large. For example, if a manager forgoes a valuable investment opportunity for personal reasons (for example, being overly risk averse), the residual loss can be significant – the potential returns to this project might have been huge. *Total agency costs* are the sum of the *out-of-pocket costs* (monitoring and bonding costs) plus the opportunity cost of the residual loss.

Incentives to Devise Efficient Contracts. Parties to a contract generally would be expected to make reasoned forecasts of the activities to be accomplished and structure contracts both to facilitate those activities and limit dysfunctional actions. At the time these contracts are negotiated, the actions motivated by the incentives established through the contracts are anticipated and reflected in their prices and terms. Hence, the agency costs in any contractual relationship are borne by the contracting parties. This means that some individual(s) always can benefit by devising ways of reducing these costs. By writing more effective contracts, the size of the pie can be increased, potentially benefitting all parties to the contract since there is more to share.

Agency Problems and Financial Contracts. Agency problems emanating from conflicts of interest in principal/agent relationships are present in virtually all cooperative activities among self-interested individuals, whether or not they occur in a hierarchical fashion. Jensen and Meckling use this agency framework to analyze the resolution of conflicts of interest among stockholders, managers, and bondholders of the firm. Since their pathbreaking work, many researchers have used agency theory and related empirical analysis to shed light on a wide variety of corporate financial policies and contracts. In this book, we employ agency theory in our analysis of capital structure decisions, corporate payout policy, and executive incentives.

1.3   SUMMARY

Corporate finance focuses on three major policies: capital budgeting policy, capital structure/financing policy, and payout policy. Prior to the mid-20th century, there was little sound theory to guide managers in any of these choices. Since that time, financial economists have produced a substantial body of theoretical models of corporate financial policies and empirical research testing those models.

At least five basic building blocks have emerged from this research, building blocks that are important for a managerially useful understanding of corporate finance. These include Efficient Market Theory, Portfolio Theory, Capital Asset Pricing Theory, Option Pricing Theory, and Agency Theory. These building blocks serve as a foundation for our analysis of corporate financial decisions in subsequent chapters.

Notes

1. Among other things, this chapter updates material found in Smith (1990).
2. While most studies present evidence that markets are Weak-Form Efficient, some studies have documented potentially exploitable patterns in stock returns. For example, there is some evidence for stock-market "momentum": where delivered superior or inferior returns over several weeks or months tend to produce similar high or low returns over subsequent weeks or months (e.g., Jegadeesh and Titman, 1993). However, the profit opportunities in exploiting these apparent patterns are both small and risky.
3. Evidence exists that the average mutual fund manager has skills in picking stocks. However, their superior returns are primarily captured through higher fees, not by the investors in these funds; generally, they earn only average risk-adjusted return after costs and fees. See Berk and Binsbergen (2015). In 2020 for the eleventh year in a row, the majority of actively managed U.S. large-cap funds underperformed the S&P 500 (Langley, Karen, "Stock Pickers Trailed Market Again in Roller Coaster 2020," *Wall Street Journal*, March 11, 2021). https://www.wsj.com/articles/stock-pickers-trailed-market-again-in-roller-coaster-2020-11615464001
4. The translation for the Bernoulli quote is from Rubinstein (2002). The origin of the eggs quote is attributed by some to Miguel de Cervantes, who wrote *Don Quixote* in the early 1600s.
5. This discussion draws on the analysis in Smith (1979).
6. The call option holder has a type of interest-free loan, which increases in value with the market interest rate and the time to maturity.

7.   This section presents a condensed summary of our more extensive discussion of agency problems in "Incentive conflicts and contracts," Brickley, Smith and Zimmerman (2021: chapter 10). Jensen and Meckling published a pathbreaking paper in 1976 that initiated research on the implications of agency theory for corporate finance. Their paper has prompted a large body of related theoretical and empirical work and has received more than 97,000 Google citations to date (August 2021).

2   Capital budgeting

Capital budgeting refers to the process a firm uses to evaluate and decide whether to pursue specific investment opportunities the firm has developed. Capital budgeting is one of the most important financial functions that firms perform – it is the process by which the assets of the firm are created and maintained. Moreover, these decisions are among the most frequently delegated to lower-level managers within the firm. This chapter presents a brief discussion of some of the major issues relating to capital budgeting.[1]

2.1   Net present value

If the question were *"Which would you rather have $1 or $2?"*, a five-year old could answer it. However, if the question is *"Which would you rather have $1 today or a promise of $2 five years from now?"*, the answer is far less clear. The ultimate purpose of discounting and net present value calculations is to make the answer to the second question as obvious as that of the first.

As in this second question, the expected cash flows of investment projects normally occur at different points in time. For example, new projects often involve a cash outlay today with the expectation of obtaining positive net cash inflows in the future. A fundamental principle in finance is that a dollar today is worth more than a dollar in the future – by investing a dollar today, you would earn interest on your investment and thus have more than a dollar in the future.

For example, if the interest rate were 10%, a dollar invested today would produce a *future value* one year from now of $1.00 x 1.10 = $1.10 (the 1.10 is simply 1 + r, where r is the interest rate = 10%). Conversely, a promised payment of $1.10 one year from now has a *present value* of $1.10/1.10 = $1.00. *Discounting* is the process of converting the future value of $1.10 to its present value of $1.00. Ten percent in this example is the *discount rate*. Calculating present values is a bit more complicated when expected future cash flows occur at multiple dates in the future and when they vary in risk. However, the basic principle is the same. The *Net Present Value* (NPV) of a given investment project is found by discounting all its future expected cash flows to their present values and then adding them together. The general formula for Net Present Value is:

$$NPV = \left[\sum_{t=0}^{\infty} E(CF_t) / (1+r) \right] - \textit{Initial Invesment Cost}]$$

(2.1)

where t is the time period (for example, year 1, year 2, and so on), $E(CF_t)$ is the expected cash flow at time t and *r* is the appropriate discount rate, given the timing and riskiness of the cash flow.

2.2   Capital budgeting decision rules

Modern finance theory maintains that within well-functioning capital markets the value of an asset, a project, or a firm as a whole is equal to the discounted present value of its expected future cash flows. Thus, in making investment decisions, managers should calculate the NPV of each feasible project. Projects with positive NPVs should be accepted; those with negative NPVs should be rejected. Surveys indicate that most corporations use NPV analysis in making capital budgeting decisions; its use is particularly high among large publicly traded companies and firms managed by CEOs with MBAs (Graham and Harvey, 2001).

Firms often supplement NPV analysis with calculations of the project's internal rate of return (IRR) – the discount rate that makes the NPV of the project's expected cash flows equal to zero. If the IRR is greater than the appropriate discount rate for the project – its cost of capital – the project has a positive NPV and should be undertaken. The IRR of a project is easy to calculate and relatively simple to communicate to others. Properly applied, IRR and NPV analysis typically produce the same decision with respect to whether a project should be accepted or not. Exceptions are more likely when the term structure of interest rates is steeply sloping, whether increasing or decreasing. But IRRs contain less information than NPVs, since IRRs do not indicate how much additional value would be created by a project. In the case of mutually exclusive projects, for instance, managers should select the one with the highest NPV, not the highest IRR, since it would produce a greater increase in firm value.

Some firms also calculate a project's *payback period* – the number of years that it is expected to take to recover the initial investment. In years past, many firms used simple *payback rules* to make investment decisions – accept a project, if and only if, the payback period is less than some specified number of years. Payback rules, however, are subject at least to two major criticisms: (1) they ignore the time value of money (interest rates) and (2) they ignore cash flows beyond the specified payback period. Nonetheless, payback rules still are used within a fair number of firms – particularly small, non-publicly traded firms and those with older CEOs without MBAs (Graham and Harvey, 2001). Despite their theoretical objections, payback periods are relatively easy to calculate and can provide useful information to cash-constrained (especially private) firms with more limited access to external capital markets. If an investment project does not generate positive cash flows in a relatively short period of time, a cash-constrained firm might go out of business before the anticipated positive cash flows arrive.

Although finance theory suggests that firms should rely primarily on NPV analysis in making capital budgeting decisions, this does not imply that managers facing actual project decisions should avoid calculating IRRs, payback periods, or other metrics used in the capital budgeting process. These supplemental measures are relatively easy to calculate, and, in some cases, can provide additional insight of use to managers. For instance, focusing attention on IRRs might motivate operating managers to search for productive ways to increase the expected returns on proposed projects.

We should note that firms that regularly use NPV analysis for project evaluation do not employ it for all investment decisions. For example, a decision to modernize an employee restroom is likely made using more subjective criteria. It is not that an NPV calculation would lead to the incorrect decision. Rather it is that although the costs are relatively easy to quantify, benefits are not. Devoting enough resources to employ a comprehensive NPV calculation would be unwise. Any benefits of a more precise estimate of the project's NPV probably are less than the costs of obtaining the information.

2.3   Cost of capital

NPV analysis consists of discounting the expected future cash flows of a proposed investment employing a discount rate that is appropriate for the timing and riskiness of its cashflows. In this process, the CFO is selecting a discount rate that reflects the investment's opportunity cost of capital.

One widely employed method to estimate this opportunity cost is to calculate the firm's *weighted average cost of capital* (WACC); it reflects the average cost of capital for the firm's existing projects. It is calculated by weighting the cost of each source of funds by its proportion of the total market value of the firm. The most common method for estimating the (opportunity) cost of equity capital is to use the CAPM (Graham and Harvey, 2001).[2]

An issue arises when the term structure of interest rates is not flat – when the interest rate for a risk-free one-year government bond differs from that of a ten-year bond, for example. One approach is to estimate the risk premium – the difference between the rate that this firm must pay and the government bond rate. This estimated risk premium is then added to the observed term structure.

Some firms use their WACCs to evaluate all potential investment projects. Generally, however, the appropriate cost of capital varies across proposed projects – some are less risky than others. Using a single WACC for all projects leads to underinvestment in projects that have low project-specific costs of capital and overinvestment in high-risk projects. One technique used to address this concern is to estimate a WACC from other firms whose average projects are similar in risk to the project under consideration. Another (less formal) method is to adjust the WACC up or down, based on an assessment of the systematic risk associated with the given project. For example, if the project is highly pro-cyclical, the WACC would be increased to reflect its higher-than-average systematic risk.

2.4   Real options

Investment projects often have embedded *real options*. For example, a heating plant might be constructed so that one could change its fuel from oil to gas simply by flipping a switch. The firm thus has the option to change from one fuel to the other as the relative prices for the two change. This option is valuable, since the firm can choose its fuel based on actual fuel prices that can change over time. Other common "real options" include the ability to time additional project-related investments, the option to abandon an unsuccessful project, and the option to expand a successful project.

Firms can use option pricing models to value real options. Graham and Harvey (2001) found that over one-fourth of their surveyed companies claimed to use real-option evaluation techniques in their capital budgeting processes. These authors were surprised by this relatively high level, given that real-option valuation techniques were relatively new at the time of the survey. Nonetheless, real-option valuation models are relatively complicated and can be difficult to use in practice. Thus, many firms primarily conduct real-option analysis on a qualitative basis, as part of its strategic planning process.

2.5   Competition and strategy

NPV analysis involves the discounting of future expected cash flows. Incorrect investment decisions occur either if managers use the wrong discount rate or if their cash-flow forecasts are of poor quality. Finance theory generally is silent on how to forecast cash flows. Yet often, the quality of the cash-flow forecast is more important than the choice of the discount rate. It matters little how precisely estimated the discount rate might be, if the cash-flow forecasts are "garbage."

Most firms operate within quite competitive environments. If a firm were making high profits today, it would be likely to draw a crowd of firms that would like a share of these profits. Even though quite profitable today, unless there are effective barriers to entry and imitation, a firm should anticipate increased competition, lower prices, and reduced profit margins in the future. It is important, therefore, for managers to consider the effects of competition in making or assessing cash-flow forecasts. Hence, if cash-flow forecasts assume that prices and profit margins will remain at current levels, managers would be well advised to question whether this assumption is likely to be valid. Considering the effects of competition is generally a critical first step in evaluating a NPV analysis and should be done before delving too deeply into specific numerical calculations.[3]

Competitive strategy focuses on the search for a favorable competitive position within an actual marketplace. Ultimately, it is the search for a strategy within an industry that potentially allows the firm to make sustainable above-average profits relative to other firms in the same industry (Porter, 2008). To meet this objective, a firm must establish a *competitive advantage* that is valuable, rare, and difficult to imitate. It is critically important that there be a close link between strategy and corporate finance. Investment decisions need to be made within the context of the firm's specific strategy. Today's CFOs are spending more time than in the past on strategic development and implementation. They bring important financial skills and tools to the planning process. According to a survey by McKinsey and Company, "two thirds of all executives agree that the best way for CFOs to ensure their company's success would be to spend more time on strategy" (Agrawal, Gibbs and Monier, 2015).

2.6   Project analysis

NPV analysis requires managers to make an array of assumptions about the future – for example, prices, costs, tax rates, government regulation, and firm production rates. Particularly for larger projects, it is important for managers to examine the robustness of their conclusions to variations in their basic assumptions. Firms often conduct *sensitivity analysis*, where key assumptions that drive future cash-flow forecasts are varied from the pessimistic to the optimistic. Mangers also can vary multiple assumptions at the same time, using *scenario analysis* (for instance, Monte Carlo simulations). If reasonable variations in key assumptions yield the same conclusion about whether the proposed project has a positive NPV, managers can be more confident that they are making a good investment decision. If its bottom line varies, with changes in key assumptions, a sensible reaction is for the firm to invest in additional information and analysis before making a final investment decision.

2.7   Summary

Net present value (NPV) analysis is the most theoretically sound technique for evaluating the merits of potential investment projects. Calculating internal rates of return (IRRs), payback periods, etc., however, is inexpensive and can provide useful additional insights in some cases.

A firm's weighted average cost of capital (WACC) reflects its average cost of capital for the firm's existing projects. Many firms use their WACC to evaluate all proposed investment projects. But the cost of capital can vary among proposed projects depending on their risk. Managers can make significant investment mistakes if they use unadjusted WACCs to evaluate projects that deviate substantially in risk from their "average project."

Many investment projects have embedded real options. Some firms use quantitative methods to evaluate these options. Many, however, consider real options in their planning effort on a more qualitative basis.

It is important for managers to consider competition from other firms when making cash-flow forecasts. They should consider the fact that prices and profit margins often drop over time as competition intensifies. Competitive strategy is the search for a favorable competitive position within an industry that would allow the firm to make sustainable above-average profits relative to other firms in the same industry. Capital budgeting should be closely linked to the firm's strategy. CFOs are spending increasing amounts of their time on strategy-related issues.

NPV analysis requires managers to make an array of assumptions that relate to the future cash flows of a project. Especially for large investment projects, it is important for managers to examine the robustness of their conclusions to variations in key assumptions that underlie their forecasts.

Notes

1. We concentrate on high-level issues in this chapter. More detailed analyses of capital budgeting are presented in most modern corporate finance textbooks; for example, Brealey, Myers and Allen (2020).

2. Within the U.S. tax code, corporations can deduct interest payments on their debt. Therefore, the after-tax cost of debt capital equals $r_d (1 - \tau)$, where r_d is the interest rate on the debt and τ is the firm's marginal tax rate. Suppose that the respective market values of the firm's debt and equity are $300 and $600, $r_d = 6\%$, $\tau = .3$ and the expected return on equity $= 10\%$. The firm's WACC $= [(600/900) \times .1] + [(300/900) \times (.06 \times (1 - .3))] = .081 = 8.1\%$. In practice, the face value of debt is often used as a proxy for its harder-to-observe market value – especially when dealing with bank debt or other private (non-traded) debt. The WACC formula seems to suggest that the firm could lower its cost of capital by replacing equity with debt, which has a lower cost. But this is not correct within a perfect capital market with no taxes or transaction costs and a fixed investment policy (Modigliani and Miller, 1958). As the firm's leverage rises, the cost of its remaining equity increases due to higher risk, which offsets the apparent advantage of the lower-cost debt (see Chapter 3).

3. More generally mangers should consider not only the threats of competition from existing rivals and potential entrants, but also the threats from (1) key suppliers who might increase their prices, (2) producers of substitute products, and (3) powerful buyers who might demand lower future prices. See Porter (2008).

3   Corporate finance within perfect capital markets

Like researchers studying scientific phenomena under idealized conditions (for instance, the assumption of a perfect vacuum in physics) financial economists have analyzed financial policy and payout policy under the idealized assumption that capital markets are "perfect." A *perfect capital market* is defined to have the following characteristics:

- There are no taxes on the firm or its investors.
- There are no transactions (or contacting, information or agency) costs.
- Firms and investors are price takers – no firm or investor can individually influence the way that the market prices securities.

While actual capital markets are not perfect, the analysis of corporate finance within the context of these idealized market conditions provides useful managerial insights. Specifically, it points us in the right direction for a more detailed understanding of those factors important in driving corporate policy decisions within the environment in which firms actually operate. It also provides insights into the valuations of a firm's debt and equity claims.

The remaining chapters in this book focus on corporate leverage and payout decisions – whether and how they affect firm value. In this chapter, we first provide an overview of the data on leverage and payout policies – the basic information that we seek to understand within this book. We then discuss corporate financial policy, security pricing, and corporate payout policy within the context of perfect capital markets. In subsequent chapters, we examine the implications of relaxing these quite stringent assumptions.

3.1   Basic data on leverage and payouts

A firm's capital structure often is summarized by its leverage ratio, which can be defined as the book value of debt divided by the sum of the book values of debt and equity. Based on data reported in Graham, Leary and Roberts (2015), Figure 3.1 displays the long-term trends in average leverage ratios for unregulated firms in the United States. During the first half of the 20th century, the average leverage for these firms was relatively low and stable (around 12%). It then increased dramatically through the 1970s to around 35%.[1] The average ratio declined somewhat during the 1990s and first decade of the 21st century but remained high relative to the first half of the 20th century.

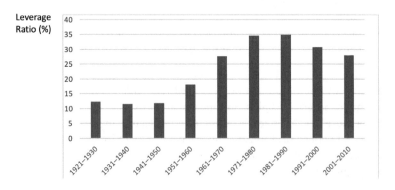

Figure 3.1   Leverage ratios of unregulated US firms by decade

This figure displays the average book leverage ratio for nonregulated US firms covered by COMPUSTAT or Moody's from the 1920s through the first decade of the 21st century. The leverage ratio = (Book Value of Debt)/(Book Value of Debt +Book Value of Equity).
Source: Based on a subset of the data originally reported in Table 1 of Graham, Leary and Roberts (2015).

There is significant cross-sectional variation in firm leverage. Lemmon, Roberts and Zender (2008) document that, in any given year, the average leverage for the top-quartile firms is about 50% higher than for the bottom quartile of firms. Some firms are highly levered, while others have little debt in their capital structures. Capital structures for individual firms tend to be relatively stable over time. Average leverage for regulated companies has been much higher and more stable through time than that for unregulated companies; for regulated firms it was around 40% or higher in all years over the 1920–2010 period (Graham, Leary and Roberts, 2015). In the remainder of this chapter as well as in Chapters 4 through 7, we present the theory and evidence on how individual firms choose their capital structures.

Firms pay cash to shareholders through both dividends and share repurchases. Share repurchases were rare prior to the early 1980s, but since the late 1990s, nonfinancial firms have paid more cash to shareholders through repurchases than dividends.[2] As depicted in Figure 3.2 (based on data reported in Floyd, Li and Skinner, 2015), the first years of the 21st century witnessed a significant increase in real cash payouts to shareholders (expressed in 2012 dollars). Firms in the S&P 1500 paid less than $400 billion to shareholders in 2000. In 2018, they paid close to $1.6 trillion (Zeng and Luk, 2020).

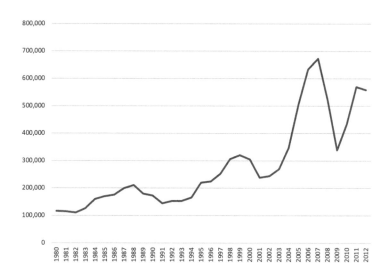

Figure 3.2   Real cash payouts to shareholders by industrial firms from 1980 to 2012

This figure displays total cash payouts (dividends and repurchases) made by public industrial companies in the COMPUSTAT database (financial and utility companies are not included). All payouts are expressed in 2012 dollars. *Source:* Based on a subset of the data originally reported in Table 1 of Floyd, Li and Skinner (2015).

During the 2011–2017 period, 42.1% of U.S. nonfinancial firms distributed no cash to shareholders through either dividends or stock repurchases, while over 23% made distrubutions to shareholders using both methods. The fraction of banks that pay cash to shareholders is much higher than for industrial firms. For example, 61.6% of the industrial firms on COMPUSTAT paid no cash to shareholders in 2012, while only 27.3% of commercial banks failed to do so (Floyd, Li and Skinner, 2015). Banks also have been more likely to pay out cash through dividends than industrial firms, which are more likely to use share repurchases. The yearly variation in cash dividends tends to be lower than for share repurchases – repurchases are more likely to be reduced during recessionary periods. For example, the big drop in cash payouts in Figure 3.2 during the December 2007 to June 2009 recession was largely driven by a decline in share repurchases. Chapter 8 examines the theory and evidence on corporate pay-out policies.

3.2   Financial policy

An important corporate decision is how to finance the firm's operations and investments. Simply cast, how much should the firm borrow versus raise in equity capital?

3.2.1   Capital structure irrelevance within perfect capital markets

Nobel laureates Franco Modigliani and Merton Miller published a path-breaking paper in 1958 that laid the foundation for a positive theory of corporate financial policy. They demonstrate that within perfect capital markets and given the firm's investment policy, the financing choice does not affect current firm value.

Basic proofs of this *Capital Structure Irrelevance Proposition* rely on arbitrage arguments: If the financing policy did affect its market value, there would be arbitrage opportunities that could be used to produce costless increases in wealth. The existence of arbitrage opportunities is inconsistent with equilibrium within a *perfect capital market*.

As the box quoting Yogi Berra suggests, the investment decision can be viewed as creating a pie of fixed size that is shared among bondholders and stockholders. In a perfect market, it does not matter how the firm divides that pie between the bondholders and stockholders. If one split is preferred to another by investors, they can rearrange their claims on the firm privately at zero cost. Thus, the firm's leverage decision is irrelevant – it cannot affect total firm value.[3]

A HALL OF FAME BASEBALL PLAYER ILLUSTRATES THE M&M IRRELEVANCE PROPOSITION

Yogi Berra was a beloved Hall of Fame catcher for the New York Yankees baseball team. He was famous for making funny, sometimes blundering, statements that came to be known as "Yogi-isms," such as *"It's like déjà vu all over again"* and *"It ain't over 'til it's over."*

One evening, Yogi went to a pizza shop and ordered a medium pizza. The waiter asked if he wanted it cut into four or eight slices. After only a moment's thought, he replied, *"You better make it four – I don't think I could eat eight."*

This "Yogi-ism" highlights the basic logic that underlies *the M&M Irrelevance Proposition.* Investment policy is fixed – one medium pizza has been made. This fixes the total amount of crust, sauce, and cheese that's available for his meal. There are no taxes, hence none of the pizza goes to the IRS. And with no transaction costs, none is lost by cutting it into either four or eight slices. In the kitchen, they use a sharp, round, pizza-cutting knife, and this one is Teflon-coated – nothing sticks to the knife. So, no matter how it is sliced, Yogi gets the entire pizza.

3.2.2   Managerial implications of M&M

Modigliani and Miller permanently changed the role of economic analysis in discussions of corporate capital structure. Now admittedly, some within the business community have looked at this M&M Proposition and concluded that it is simply academic musing, of no real use to those corporate officers responsible for financing decisions in their own firms operating within actual markets. They argue:

> No taxes! Where could I operate with no taxes? Nowhere on this planet! No contracting costs! The investment bankers and securities lawyers that I deal

with would not work for their mothers without a fee. And we are supposed to hold investment policy fixed. What does that even mean? This is just a bunch of useless academic hogwash!

Now admittedly, M&M's analysis provides little or no explanation for the corporate financing policies observed in practice. And the way they stated their result on its face seems of little managerial import. But it does tell us what might matter – it tells us where to look. If we restate it in a different, but logically equivalent, way its managerial implications become clear:[4]

> If the choice of corporate financing policy does affect the current market value of the firm, it must do so in at least one of only three ways:
> 1. By changing the tax liabilities of either the firm or its security holders.
> 2. By changing the firm's contracting, transactions, information, or bankruptcy costs.
> 3. By affecting the firm's incentives with respect to its choice of investment decisions either immediately or in the future.

Actual capital markets are not perfect – taxes and contracting costs clearly exist. There is now a large body of theoretical and empirical research on how these factors can affect a firm's financial structure. While we still do not have a comprehensive theory to explain all aspects of the capital structure decision, we know much more than we did prior to M&M. In subsequent chapters, we rely on this literature to provide useful managerial insights regarding decisions about corporate capital structure and financial policy.

3.2.3   Valuing corporate securities[5]

With perfect markets and given the firm's investment policy, the M&M analysis implies that the firm's choice of capital structure is irrelevant – any capital structure leaves firm value unchanged. However, within this context, something that still can be analyzed is the valuation of the firm's debt and equity claims. Black and Scholes (1973), following a suggestion by Jack Treynor, argue that the option pricing model can be employed to value the debt and equity of a simple levered firm. Specifically, they assume that: (1) The firm issues pure-discount (zero-coupon) bonds that include a covenant prohibiting any dividend payments to shareholders until after the bondholders have been repaid. (2) The bonds mature at time t^*, T time periods from now, at which time the bondholders are paid (if possible), with any residual paid to the stockholders. If at maturity, the assets of the firm are insufficient to pay the bondholders what they were promised, the bondholders get the firm's assets, and consequently the stockholders get nothing. (3) The firm's investment policy is fixed. (4) Finally, they make the technical assumption that the distribution of the potential values of the firm's assets at the end of any finite time interval is lognormal with a constant variance rate.

In essence, issuing zero-coupon bonds is equivalent to the stockholders selling the assets of the firm to the bondholders for the proceeds of the bond issue plus a call option to repurchase the assets from the bondholders with an exercise price equal to the face value of the bonds. Figure 3.3 illustrates the payoffs to both the equity holders and bondholders for each potential value of the firm's assets at the maturity date of the bonds. Under these assumptions, the equity of the firm is like a call option. Applying the Black-Scholes option pricing formula yields:

$$E = VN \left\{ \frac{\ln(V/F) + (r + \sigma^2/2)T}{\sigma\sqrt{T}} \right\}$$

$$-e^{-rT} FN \left\{ \frac{\ln(V/F) + (r - \sigma^2/2)T}{\sigma\sqrt{T}} \right\}$$

$$(3.1)$$

where E is the value of the firm's equity, V is the current market value of the firm's assets, F is the face value of the firm's zero-coupon bonds, σ^2 is the variance rate on V, T is the time to maturity of the bonds (t*-t), r is the risk-free rate of interest, and N{z} is the cumulative standard normal distribution from minus infinity to z.

In their analysis of the pricing of options, Black and Scholes were interested in valuing options that were priced and traded in capital markets. But here, we are interested in employing this analogy between the payoffs to an option with the payoff to the equity holders of this simple levered firm. The case where this analogy is exact is quite special, and thus the circumstances where this specific functional form is exact are extremely rare. Nonetheless, the general insights from this analysis are quite broadly relevant. Thus, we will focus on the general form implications:

$$V = E\left(\overset{+}{V},\overset{-}{F},\overset{+}{T},\overset{+}{\sigma^2},\overset{+}{r}\right) + B\left(\overset{+}{V},\overset{+}{F},\overset{-}{T},\overset{-}{\sigma^2},\overset{-}{r}\right)$$

(3.2)

where the signs above the independent variables indicate their partial effects; for example, $E\left(\overset{+}{V},...\right)$ means $\partial E / \partial V > 0$ [that is, holding other variables constant, an increase (decrease) in firm value will cause an increase (decrease) in the value of the firm's equity].

These partial effects are in the expected direction and have quite intuitive interpretations: An increase in firm value shifts the entire distribution of future asset values to the right. This increases the coverage on the firm's bonds, lowering the probability of default, thereby increasing their value; what is left for the equity holders also increases. You simply cannot hurt the interest of any of the firm's claimholders by increasing the size of the pie.

Because we are examining partial effects, we hold the other right-hand-side variables fixed – including the current market value of the assets. Thus, given the value of the assets, something that increases the current market value of the bonds must reduce the value of the equity. Therefore, increasing the face value of the bonds increases the bondholders claim on the firm's assets, and increases the value of the bonds. But given the value of the firm's assets, this increase in the value of the bonds must reduce the value of the firm's equity. Increasing either the time to maturity of the bonds or in the risk-free interest rate lowers the present value of the face value of the bonds, lowering their current market value. Again, given the value of the assets, this must increase the current market value of the equity. Finally, an increase in either the time to maturity of the bonds or the variance rate of the assets increases the dispersion of possible values of the firm's assets at the maturity of the bonds. Since the bondholders have a maximum payment (F) which they can receive, an increase in the dispersion of possible outcomes increases the probability that the value of the firm's assets will be below the face value of the bonds, increasing the probability of default, and lowering the value of the bonds. But given the

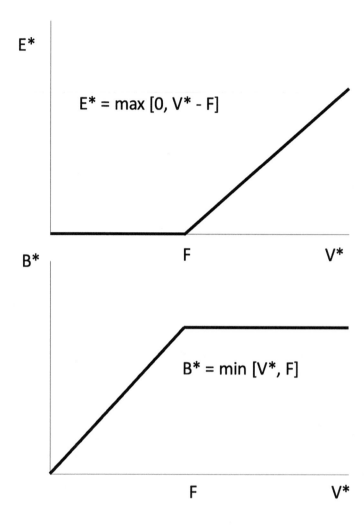

Figure 3.3   Debt and equity values on the maturity date of the debt

This figure shows 1) the dollar payoff to equity of the firm on the maturity date of its bonds with face value F, as a function of the value of the assets (V*): E* = max [0, V- F.] and 2) the dollar payoff of the bonds on their maturity date as a function of the value of the firm's assets: B* = min [V*, F] value of the assets, something that reduces the value of the bonds must increase the value of the equity.

3.2.4   The option pricing model and the CAPM

In Chapter 1, we discussed the Capital Asset Pricing Model (CAPM) and how it has been used to describe equilibrium security prices within a single period setting with no taxes and the assumption that investors can borrow and lend at the risk-free rate. The pricing of debt and equity employing the option pricing model, described above, is consistent with the continuous-time version of the CAPM.[6] Analogous to its single-period counterpart, the continuous-time CAPM implies that the equilibrium expected rate of return to an asset at every point in time is:

$$r_j = r + \beta_j \left(r_m - r \right)$$

(3.3)

where r_m is the instantaneous expected return to the market portfolio, and $\beta_j = \left(cov(r_j, r_m) / \sigma^2(r_m) \right)$ measures the systematic risk of security j.

It is relatively easy to show that within this model: (1) Even if the systematic risk of the firm's assets, β_v, were constant, the risk of its equity, β_E, will not be. It changes with either a change in the value of the assets or the time to maturity of the bonds. (2) Since the elasticity of the value of the equity with respect to the firm's assets is greater than one, the systematic risk of the stock is greater than the systematic risk of the firm's assets.[7] (3) Conversely, the systematic risk of the debt is less than the systematic risk of the firm's assets. (4) As we noted in Chapter 2, prospective projects can be viewed as options. This analysis thus implies that after the project is completed, its asset risk is less – that is, it has a lower beta – than the project has as a prospective growth opportunity.

3.2.5   Risk structure of interest rates

The *yield to maturity (YTM)* of a bond is the rate of return to a bond held to maturity, assuming all promised payments are made. In other words, it is the discount rate, $\hat{r}$, that equates promised future payments to the bond's current price. For example, consider a two-year zero-coupon bond with a face value of $1,000 with a current market price of $826.45. The YTM of the bond, $\hat{r}$, would be:

$$\$826.45\left(1+\hat{r}\right)^2 = \$1,000$$

$$\hat{r} = 10\%$$

There is an inverse relation between bond prices and YTMs – the lower the price, the higher the yield. The risk-free rate, r, is the YTM of a default-free government bond. The nominal risk-free rate (what you can infer from prices observed in the marketplace) depends on the expected inflation rate and the supply and demand for funds. Corporate bonds, which have some probability of default, have higher YTMs. The risk premium is defined as $\hat{r}-r$.

Nobel laureate Robert Merton (1974) suggests that since discussions of bond pricing frequently employ yields rather than bond prices, it can be convenient to transform the bond value in equation (3.2) into an excess return.

Let the promised yield to maturity of a risky corporate bond with T periods remaining (assuming it does not default), where $\hat{r}(T)$ is defined by:[8]

$$e^{\hat{r}(T)\bullet T} = F / B$$

(3.4)

Then the risk premium on risky corporate debt can be measured by

$$\hat{r}(T)-r = \left(\ln(F / B)/T\right)-r$$

(3.5)

This implicitly defines a risk structure of interest rates.

Because of the relation between the value of the bonds and the other variables in the model, this risk structure also can be expressed in terms of these variables:

$$\hat{r} = \hat{r}(\overset{-}{V}, \overset{+}{F}, \overset{?}{T}, \overset{+}{\sigma^2}, \overset{+}{r})$$

(3.6)

The interpretation of the effects on the promised interest rate of the value of the assets, the variance rate, and the risk-free rate are straightforward – those values which increase the value of the bonds reduce the promised interest rate. There is a less than proportional increase in the value of the bonds from an increase in the face value of the bonds because of an increased probability of default; thus, the promised interest rate rises. There are two effects on the promised interest rate of the time to maturity, either of which can dominate: (1) an increase in the time to maturity lowers the (zero-coupon) bond price, and thus raises the promised interest rate; but (2) it increases the denominator of the first term [ln(F/B)/T], lowering the promised interest rate.

3.3   Payout policy

Another important financial decision involves the firm's payout policy. Simply cast, how much cash, if any, should the firm payout to its shareholders? And should these payouts be made through a dividend payment or share repurchase?

3.3.1   Payout policy irrelevance within perfect capital markets

Miller and Modigliani (1961) extend their analysis of capital structure to dividend policy.[9] They argue that within perfect capital markets if corporate investment policy is fixed, then the firm's choice of payout policy leaves the current market value of the firm unaffected. (Note that adhering to an investment policy such as *We will take all positive NPV projects and reject all negative NPV projects* is sufficient. What is necessary is that investment policy and payout policy are independent of each other at each point in time.)

The intuition behind the *M&M Dividend Irrelevance Proposition* lies in the idea that within a perfect capital market the value of a firm is determined by its investment policy. Individuals who desire cash in the current period can obtain it by selling shares in the company, while those wanting to invest for the future can use cash distributions to buy more shares. Since individual investors can create any desired cash flow pattern on their own, firm value is unaffected by any specific payout policy that the firm might choose.[10] In Chapter 8, we present a more detailed explanation and example to illustrate these concepts.

3.3.2   Payouts financed through asset liquidations

The M&M Dividend Irrelevance Proposition assumes payouts to equity holders are financed by selling new shares. However, if the dividends were financed by liquidating some of the firm's assets (or out of internally generated cash flows), such payouts will affect the value of the firm's outstanding equity and bonds. Following Merton (1973), applying option pricing analysis yields:

$$V = E(\overset{+}{V},\overset{-}{F},\overset{+}{T},\overset{+}{\sigma^2},\overset{+}{r},\overset{+}{d}) + B(\overset{+}{V},\overset{+}{F},\overset{-}{T},\overset{-}{\sigma^2},\overset{-}{r},\overset{-}{d})$$

(3.7)

Higher dividends financed by liquidating the firm's assets reduces the coverage on its bonds, increases the probability of default, and thus reduces their value. Given the current market value of the firm's assets, anything that reduces the current market value of the debt increases the value of the equity. (Note that the lower future asset value also lowers the expected future value of the equity, but the present values of the dividend payments are greater than this reduction in the expected future value.)

3.3.3   Toward an optimal payout policy

Restating the M&M Dividend Irrelevance Proposition (as we did their Capital Structure Irrelevance Proposition) implies that if payout policy is to matter it must be due to a violation of either the assumption of perfect capital markets or the assumption of a fixed investment policy. Questions concerning *Why firms pay dividends?* and *What are the effects of alternative payout policies when the firm cash-flow distributions are allowed to vary with payout policy?* have continued to be a source of much debate and empirical examination. We postpone the analysis of these questions until Chapter 8, where we discuss the relevant literature in more detail and provide managerial insights about corporate payout policy.

3.4   Summary

The M&M Capital Structure and Dividend Irrelevance Propositions are arguably the most important ideas in all corporate finance. This is not because capital structure and payout decisions are likely to be irrelevant within the actual firms and markets within which managers might operate. Rather, their importance lies in guiding us in where to look. If financing or payout decisions affect firm value, there must be some differential tax implications for the firm or its investors, or some difference in relevant costs, or some important interdependence between the firm's choice of financing or payout policy and either the firm's current or future investment policy.

Within their idealized environment, the M&M Irrelevance Proposition tells us nothing about optimal financing or payout policies. But there are useful insights into how the debt and equity claims are priced. We employ the Black and Scholes option pricing model to value the debt and equity of a simple levered firm. Increases in the value of the firm's assets increase the values of both the firm's equity and debt. Given the value of the firm's assets, anything that increases the value of the firm's debt causes an equally sized reduction in the value of the firm's equity. We restate the bond pricing results in terms of promised interest rates. We also examine the implications of this pricing for the interaction with the continuous time capital asset pricing model.

Notes

1. The dramatic increase in the average leverage ratio started around 1946 in the aftermath of WW2.
2. Much of the data discussed in this chapter is from Standard and Poor's Compustat, as summarized in Brealey, Myers and Allen (2020) and other cited papers.
3. Note that one might think of the M&M Proposition as a special case of the *Coase Theorem*. Nobel laureate Ronald Coase argued that with no contracting costs (as well as a few other assumptions), the allocation of property rights has no effect on the overall production decisions that are made, and

thus it will not affect the total wealth created. It will, however, affect the allocation of wealth among the market participants. But since M&M was published in 1958 and the Coase Theorem was published in 1960, it might be more appropriate to call Coase's work a generalization of M&M. However, it's not quite that simple; some of his important underlying concepts, such as the importance of transaction costs in making economic organization relevant, are published in Coase (1937) – so in this sense, M&M as a special case of Coase also works.

4. A logic course (from either the math or philosophy department) should convince you that two statements, although appearing different, might in fact be logically equivalent. For example, this M&M Proposition is basically of the form: *If A is true, then B is true.* A logically equivalent statement is: *If B is not true, then A is not true.* Here, we simply restate this M&M Proposition in this second form.

5. This section draws on a discussion in Smith (1979). It is useful, but not essential, for the reader to have a basic knowledge of algebra and introductory calculus for the remainder of section 3.2. We stress the intuition throughout, so that all readers can gain the basic insights.

6. Continuous time models view time as consisting of a series of infinitesimally short periods. Discrete time models, in contrast, divide time into distinct points, for example year 1, year 2, and so on. The simplest version of the CAPM (discussed in Chapter 1) assumes a single discrete time period.

7. The beta of the equity can be expressed as the elasticity of the value of the equity with respect to the value of the firm's assets, $\varepsilon(E,V)$, multiplied by the beta of the assets, $\beta_v : \beta_E = \varepsilon(E,V)\beta_v$ where $\varepsilon(E,V) = \dfrac{\partial E}{\partial V}\dfrac{V}{E}$. An elasticity is a measure of one variable's sensitivity to a percentage change in another variable. For example, if a one percent change in V results in a 1.5 percent change in E, the elasticity is 1.5/1 = 1.5.

8. With discrete time discounting (as used in Chapter 2): $B = F / \left(1 + \hat{r}\right)^T$ and so $\left(1 + \hat{r}\right)^T = F / B.$ Equation 3.4 is the continuous time equivalent, where $e^{r(T)*T}$ is the discount factor.

9. In the 1960s, few companies repurchased shares. Therefore, Miller and Modigliani (1961) focus their analysis on dividend policy. However, their irrelevance proposition can easily be extended to share repurchases, which now are much more common.

10. This idea is closely related to arguments by Irving Fisher (1930) who focused on interest rates and the opportunities capital markets offered individuals to disengage the timing of their consumption from their pattern of income receipts over time. Although Fisher did pathbreaking work on interest rates and capital markets – work that prompted its members to elect him President of the American Economic Association in 1929 – his work had little impact on business schools until it was "rediscovered" decades later.

4 Capital structure: taxes and bankruptcy costs[1]

As discussed in Chapter 3, the M&M Proposition asserts that, under a restrictive set of conditions – the existence of *perfect markets* and fixed investment policy – a company's financing policy does not affect its current market value. That value is determined solely by managerial decisions affecting the asset side of the (economic) balance sheet – that is, by the entire range of corporate strategic planning, capital expenditure, and operating decisions, which finance professors refer to collectively as "investment policy". If capital structure decisions affect firm value, it must be due to something that M&M assumed away – taxes, contracting costs, or interdependencies between financing and investment decisions. Following the publication of M&M (1958), among the first to be considered in the finance literature are taxes paid by issuers and investors and the costs associated with bankruptcy, or more generally with financial distress.

Under some circumstances, taxes can produce benefits from using more debt in a firm's capital structure, while the increased likelihood of financial distress imposes a cost. The *Tradeoff Theory* argues that the incremental costs and benefits associated with increased leverage can result in an optimal target capital structure, which can vary across firms and time. This chapter focuses on taxes and bankruptcy costs. In the next chapter, we discuss additional costs and benefits of debt, which augment this analysis.

4.1 Taxes and capital structure

4.1.1 Corporate taxes

The value of a company should reflect the present value of its pre-tax operating cash flows minus all associated taxes. Since a company's leverage choice affects tax liabilities at the corporate level, capital structure decisions have tax consequences that can affect firm value. The basic tax on corporate profits allows the deduction of interest payments (but not dividends) in the calculation of taxable income. Thus, the choice between debt and equity financing has potentially important consequences for the distribution of the firm's after-tax cash flows. In what academics regularly refer to as *The Tax Correction Paper*, Miller and Modigliani (1963) argue that increasing the amount of debt in a company's capital structure increases interest expense, lowers reported taxable income, lowers its expected tax liability, and thereby increases its after-tax cash flow and market value.

To examine this, let's return to Yogi's pizza-cutting example discussed in Chapter 3. Consider two firms whose investment policies are identical. Picture the (total pre-tax) values of both firms as identical medium pizzas. Each pizza can be cut into three "slices": (1) a slice for the equity holders, (2) a slice for the bondholders, and (3) a slice for the Internal Revenue Service. The equity holders slice reflects the present value of future stockholder payouts, the bondholders' slice reflects the present value of interest payments and principal repayment, and the IRS's slice reflects the present value of the firm's corporate tax liabilities. Suppose that the first firm uses less debt than the second. Because the U.S. tax code allows corporations to deduct interest payments, by including more debt in the firm's capital structure, the IRS's slice of the second firm pizza is smaller than that for the first.

Now it is important to recognize the difference between the stock or bond slices and the tax slice. To receive either the stockholders' or bondholders' slices, investors have to buy those securities. But the government receives its slice because they make the rules (the tax code), and they have prisons for those who run foul of the tax code. By including debt in the firm's capital structure, a firm reduces the size of the slice that goes to the government, thus increasing the size of the slices that can be sold to investors.[2]

Given this realization, what should a CFO do? Sell more bonds! At what point should the CFO stop? Only after one of two conditions are met: (1) There is enough debt in the firm's capital structure to drive the firm's tax obligation to zero (after that point, adding more debt creates no additional benefit). (2) Bond sales have created what is essentially an all-debt firm – you simply cannot exceed 100% debt.

Were corporate taxes the only important thing that M&M assumed away in their original paper, there would be a benefit to higher leverage. But within that model, there is no offsetting cost. Yet most corporations both operate with substantial amounts of equity in their capital structures and pay taxes. We can be confident, therefore, that it would be inappropriate to stop here in our search for an explanation for observed capital structures – there simply must be some countervailing cost of debt to explain these observations.

4.1.2   Investor-borne taxes

Miller (1977), in his Presidential Address to the American Finance Association, argues that their analysis in the tax correction paper overstates the tax advantage of debt by considering only the corporate profits tax – they ignore the income taxes paid by the firm's investors. To picture this, return to Yogi's pizza. As before, consider two otherwise identical pizzas, reflecting the present value of the firm's before-tax cash flows. But this time it is cut into four slices: (1) the stockholders' slice, (2) the bondholders' slice, (3) the IRS's slice from corporate tax payments, and (4) the IRS's slice from tax payments by investors in the firm's securities. As before, if the second firm were to put more debt in its capital structure than the first, its interest payments are higher, its taxable income is lower, and thus its corporate tax liability is lower.

But historically, corporate equity claims have been taxed on more favorable terms at the investor level than corporate debt for most investors.[3] Investors receiving interest income must pay tax on that income at ordinary income tax rates in the year in which it is received. By contrast, investors' equity income comes in two forms: dividends and capital gains. Under the current U.S. tax code, dividend income receives more favorable tax treatment than interest income. Moreover, taxes on capital gains are due only when the gain is established by selling the shares. Thus, a shareholder can postpone the payment of tax on that capital gain simply by continuing to hold the stock, thereby not realizing the gain. (And because of the "step-up in basis" that occurs at death, if the gain is postponed into the stockholder's estate, the capital gain tax liability disappears altogether.) Therefore, additional interest expense lowers the firm's corporate tax obligations, but it also increases the taxes paid by investors: Higher interest payments reduce the IRS's corporate tax slice but increase its investor tax slice.

Because investors understandably care about after-tax returns, they require compensation for their higher taxes, and this comes in the form of higher yields on corporate debt. For example, yields on tax-exempt municipal bonds are lower than those on (taxable) corporate debt of comparable risk. Investors anticipate the additional tax obligations of taxable bonds and demand higher yields to value the bonds appropriately. It is in this sense that the firm ultimately bears all of the tax consequences of its operations, whether it pays those taxes directly (in the form of corporate income taxes) or indirectly (in the form of higher promised rates of return on the bonds its sells). Given the details of the model that Miller constructed, there is an optimal amount of debt for the entire economy, but the leverage choice for any individual firm is irrelevant.[4]

DeAngelo and Masulis (1980) argue that Miller's characterization of the tax code is too simple. The extent to which a company benefits from its interest tax shields, they argue, depends on the firm's effective marginal tax rate, and tax rates vary across firms. Historically, there has been a modest amount of statutory progressivity in the corporate profits tax.[5] There are limitations on the use of other tax shields (such as investment tax credits [ITCs], foreign tax credits or tax loss carryforwards) that depend on the firm's taxable income. Thus, the firm's effective marginal tax rate also depends on whether it has other tax shields. Other things being equal, the value of a firm's interest tax shields depends on whether it has these other tax shields; a firm with more non-interest tax shields should have lower leverage ratios to reflect the reduced value of its interest tax shields.

To illustrate this point, consider two firms: The first firm is in heavy manufacturing; it regularly purchases equipment that generates ITCs. The second is in the service sector; its major expenses are for labor and hence has few ITCs. With more ITCs, the first firm has a comparative disadvantage in fully using deductions from its interest expense: more debt and more interest expense would reduce the firm's taxable income and potentially reduces its ability to deduct its ITCs.[6] With few ITCs, the second firm is better positioned to use these deductions. Thus, this tax argument implies that the firm in the service industry should have high leverage, and the firm in heavy manufacturing should have low leverage. But even a quick look at the data indicates that this is backwards. Does this mean that Miller, DeAngelo and Masulis are incorrect in their analysis? No! Their logic is flawless. Rather, it just means that other factors that we have yet to include in our analysis are quantitatively more important than these tax effects.

In sum, the tax advantage of corporate debt is almost certainly not the full statutory federal corporate tax rate (or more if we also consider state and local corporate profits taxes) for every dollar of debt, as some debt enthusiasts argue. But neither is it likely to be zero. For this reason, a consistently profitable company with few non-interest tax shields that volunteers to pay more taxes by maintaining lots of unused "debt capacity" might be leaving substantial value on the table. However, as we will discuss, there are other potentially offsetting factors to consider.

4.2   Bankruptcy costs

4.2.1   Direct bankruptcy costs

Following the 1963 publication of M&M's Tax Correction Paper, scholars searched for an offsetting cost. Among the first costs of debt to be considered were *direct bankruptcy costs* – basically out-of-pocket payments to lawyers to handle a firm's bankruptcy filing. Admittedly, this seems an odd obsession with lawyers, but it was driven in large part by Miller's insistence that:

> We must hold investment policy fixed. We already know that investment policy matters – take positive NPV projects and firm value goes up; take negative ones and it goes down. So, the fundamental question is: Given investment policy, does financing policy matter?

In order to satisfy Miller's admonition that investment policy be held fixed, these contingent payments to bankruptcy lawyers were the main thing that scholars could identify that would meet this challenge.

To picture this addition to the debate, let's again return to Yogi's pizza. Two identical medium pizzas are side by side, again both cut into four slices. The first three slices are for the stockholders, the bondholders, and the IRS corporate tax slice.[7] The fourth slice is for the bankruptcy lawyers. Now if the second pizza is sliced with a larger slice for the bondholders, as before, the IRS's slice is reduced. But now, with more debt, the probability of bankruptcy increases and so the lawyer's slice gets larger, reflecting the greater likelihood of the bankruptcy filing and their higher expected legal fees. (Note that in this discussion, the size of the legal fees if the firm files for bankruptcy does not change, just the probability that they are incurred by the firm.)

Soon after this idea was suggested as a "fix," scholars debated whether direct bankruptcy costs could possibly be large enough to offset the corporate tax advantage of debt (which some argued was as high as the firm's marginal tax rate times its total debt). An early attempt to resolve this question was by Baxter (1967), who examined a sample of filings with the bankruptcy court. He concluded that these costs were substantial. Admittedly, there were potential problems with his study. Most of the filings were by individuals and small businesses, not large public corporations. Moreover, the data that he had was limited to that supplied in the filings. Nonetheless based on his analysis, Baxter concluded that direct bankruptcy costs were 20% of the value of the firm's assets. (Publications by Stanley and Girth [1971] and Van Horne [1974] reported similar estimates.) Although Baxter recognized the limitations of his analysis, he concluded that "for corporate cases ... the costs may average a somewhat smaller percentage ... but are far from insignificant."

That was pretty much where things stood until Jerry Warner learned that bankrupt railroads must file an annual form with the Interstate Commerce Commission that includes the amount spent on lawyers to handle the firm's bankruptcy case and associated responsibilities. Warner recognized that this data was not "perfect": Rather than Chapter 11, railroads file under Chapter 77 (although the process is similar); they are regulated; and there were only 11 of these bankrupt railroads. But, of course, if they had been unregulated, they would not have been required to fill out the forms and disclose these expenditures. Ultimately Warner (1977) concluded that observations on 11 large public corporations that have gone through the bankruptcy process are better than those employed in any earlier work. So rather than dwell on its limitations, he decided to see what he could glean from this data. His study of these 11 railroads that declared bankruptcy over the period 1930–1955 indicates that the out-of-pocket expenses associated with the administration of the bankruptcy process are quite small relative to the market values of the companies in the years preceding the filing – less than 1% for these firms.

Of course, the number that a CFO would like to have in managing the tradeoff between out-of-pocket bankruptcy costs and the value of corporate interest tax shields would be the present value of the expected bankruptcy costs. From this perspective, Warner's estimates are biased: (1) He simply summed the reported costs. This procedure effectively presumes that the probability of a bankruptcy filing is 100%. The correct probability obviously is less. (2) The reported numbers should be discounted to their present values. His calculation presumes that the discount rate is zero. The correct discount rate clearly is higher. He recognized that both of these factors imply that his estimate is too high – yet it still averaged less than 1%.

For smaller companies, it is true, direct bankruptcy costs are a considerably larger fraction of firm value (about five times as large in Warner's sample). Thus, there are "scale economies" with respect to *direct* bankruptcy costs that imply that larger companies, all else being equal, should have higher leverage ratios than smaller firms. But even these higher estimates of direct bankruptcy costs, when weighted by the probability of having to file for bankruptcy in the first place, produce *expected costs* that appear far too small to make them the driving factor in major corporate financial decisions.

Miller (1977) quips that the then standard explanation of balancing the advantage of the corporate interest tax shield with the expected costs of bankruptcy sounds like the recipe for horse and rabbit stew: "Bring a large kettle of water to a rolling boil, add one horse and one rabbit, then cook until the flavors blend." The biggest problem with this dish, he argues, is that it tastes like horse stew. Miller concludes, given Warner's evidence, that the rabbit of expected direct bankruptcy costs would be incapable of balancing the horse of the corporate interest tax shield.

4.2.2   Indirect costs of financial distress

Other things being equal, highly levered firms are more likely to become financially distressed due to their higher levels of contractually obligated interest payments. Financial distress has the potential to impose large costs on a company even if the firm avoids a formal bankruptcy filing. (As in a game of horseshoes or hand-grenade throwing, when discussing corporate bankruptcy, close counts!)

First, a firm might forgo investing in positive NPV projects to preserve sufficient cash to meet required payments to lenders. Such a firm also might reduce value-increasing expenditures on such things as advertising, marketing, travel, and research and development. Therefore, in contrast to the M&M assumptions, the amount of debt in the firm's capital structure can affect its investment decisions – this in turn would reduce the overall size of the pie. Zingales (1998) examined U.S. trucking companies during the period in which they were deregulated. He found that more highly levered firms were less likely to undertake additional investment or engage in restructuring; thereafter, these firms were more likely to exit the industry.

Second, customers and suppliers become less likely to do business with a company as it becomes financially distressed. For example, customers are more reluctant to purchase products if they fear that the company will go bankrupt and fail to honor its product warranties or fail to maintain an inventory of replacement parts if the product breaks. Also, if product quality is difficult to observe prior to purchase, customers' assessment of quality might fall, reducing the price they would be willing to pay for the product. Suppliers may become less likely to enter into contracts with the firm, invest in specialized tools to make products for it, and to extend the firm trade credit. Productive employees might quit and take jobs at more stable companies.

Third, managerial time is a finite resource. If managers allocate time to appease angry creditors and disgruntled customers, figuring out ways to avoid bankruptcy, et cetera, they have less time to spend on other potentially value-increasing activities.

In the next chapter, we discuss potential conflicts of interest between bondholders and stockholders. These conflicts have the potential to impose significant (indirect) costs on a firm, particularly if it is in financial distress.

Although it is difficult for researchers to provide numerical estimates of these indirect costs of financial distress, it is reasonable to conclude that they are likely to be large relative to the expected direct costs of bankruptcy. If so, they will be a more important consideration in capital structure decisions.

4.2.3   Financial distress costs depend on asset type

The expected costs of financial distress are likely to depend on whether the firm's assets are primarily tangible (for example, plants, property, and equipment) or intangible (for example, growth opportunities, customer goodwill, and reputation). A firm whose value consists primarily of assets in place (tangible assets) is more likely to face smaller indirect costs from financial distress – its assets can simply be sold in the marketplace to pay creditors in the case of default.[8] A firm, whose value primarily reflects that of its intangible assets, can face large financial distress costs, for example, from forgoing positive NPV projects to pay creditors and loss of customer and supplier goodwill. This analysis suggests that all else being equal, firms that consist primarily of tangible assets ("assets in place") will use more debt in their capital structures than firms whose values primarily reflect those of intangible assets. This prediction is reinforced by the analysis in the next chapter of the *Underinvestment* and *Overinvestment Problems*.

It is important to note that expected financial distress costs are equal to the likelihood that the firm will become financially distressed multiplied by the costs if it does. Prominent firms, such as Microsoft, may face a small probability of financial distress, yet quite reasonably might limit the amount of debt in their capital structures because financial distress costs would be particularly high. For example, in the spring of 2021 Microsoft had but $72 billion in long-term debt compared to a market value of its equity exceeding $1.5 trillion. Microsoft presumably had the capacity to issue more debt to reduce its tax bill (reported at $8.8 billion in 2020). However, the concern about large financial distress costs is one potential reason for why this company has refrained from issuing more debt. Other possible reasons are discussed later in this book.

4.3   Summary

The M&M Proposition implies that if capital structure is to affect firm value, it must do so because of market imperfections or interdependencies between the firm's financing and investment policies. This chapter focused on two imperfections: Taxes and bankruptcy costs.

The deductibility of interest payments on bonds at the corporate level gives debt financing a potential advantage over equity financing; it reduces the taxes that the firm has to pay to the government. But tax disadvantages of debt at the investor level can offset this advantage. Firm and investors vary significantly in effective marginal tax rates, which further complicates the analysis. Ultimately, it is likely that there are tax advantages for at least some firms in including debt within their capital structures.

Potentially offsetting costs of debt financing are bankruptcy costs (or more generally the costs of financial distress). Empirical studies suggest that expected direct bankruptcy costs (for example, payments to lawyers) are likely to be small for most public corporations. However, indirect costs of financial distress (for example, from a reduced willingness by customers and suppliers to do business with the firm) are potentially quite large. Financial distress thus can produce interdependencies between financing and investment decisions that reduce firm value. Financial distress costs are more likely to be large for firms that consist primarily of intangible assets (for example, growth opportunities, customer goodwill, and reputational capital).

The *Tradeoff Theory* argues that the incremental costs and benefits associated with increased debt financing can result in an optimal target capital structure, a structure that varies across firms and time. In this chapter, we examine potential benefits and costs that derive from the tax structure, as well as costs of financial distress. In the next chapter, we consider additional costs and benefits that arise from agency conflicts.

Notes

1. This chapter draws on and updates material originally published in Barclay, Smith and Watts (1995) among other things.
2. In the U.S., courts have held that arranging one's affairs so that one's tax liability is reduced generally is legal, although limitations exist. In other countries, tax laws vary. Thus, it is important to understand the details of the local tax code wherever one might be doing business.
3. Investor tax rates vary considerably. There is a substantial amount of progressivity in the personal tax code and under President George W. Bush tax rates were reduced on qualifying dividends to a level below ordinary income tax rates. Additionally, there are groups of investors who enjoy special tax treatment. As examples, income tax rates of not-for-profit organizations, like

charities and universities, generally are zero. There also is no difference in the taxation of dividends and capital gains in pension accounts (withdrawals are taxed at ordinary tax rates when funds are distributed). And under the Japanese tax code, tax rates on dividends for investors – including those investing in U.S. securities – are zero.

4.   This is like the competitive equilibrium in an industry with many identical producers; there is an equilibrium price and quantity for the industry; each firm operates where its marginal cost (as well as long-run average cost) equals the price. But if demand were to fall, there would be exit from the industry – but with identical suppliers we cannot tell which will leave.

5.   The major "kink" in the corporate tax function is between positive versus negative taxable income – although this effect on progressivity is dampened by tax-loss carrybacks and carryforwards.

6.   For example, when ITCs were originally introduced to the tax code, they could be used to offset up to 50% of a firm's tax liabilities. Although unused ITCs can be carried forward, the IRS does not pay interest on them. Thus, the present value of these tax credits is reduced if they are not used currently.

7.   Note that this analysis predated Miller (1977), and so for now we will ignore the IRS's slice from corporate investors.

8.   These costs also can vary; for example, by how firm-specific or location-specific the firm's tangible assets are. Assets that are more specialized are of interest to fewer potential buyers and thus represent poorer collateral for lenders (see Nyatee, 2021).

5 Agency and information-related costs: capital-structure implications

As we discussed in Chapter 1, a firm can be characterized as the focal point for a set of contracts where the firm is a party to each contract. Some of these contracts may be explicit (you can show them to a judge who can force compliance), while others are only implicit. Incentive conflicts among the contracting parties generate agency costs (expenditures to control agency problems plus the residual loss from their incomplete control). Managers need to consider these costs when making financial decisions. We begin this chapter by discussing incentive conflicts among stockholders, bondholders, and managers, and the associated implications for capital structure. We then move on to discuss more generally how informational disparities between managers and outside investors can affect financing decisions. Among other things, we present the Signaling, Pecking Order, and Market-Timing theories of financial policy, which are based on these disparities.

5.1   Bondholder-stockholder conflicts

We first discuss potential conflicts of interest that can arise between stockholders and bondholders. For our purposes in this initial discussion, we assume that managers (the primary decision makers within most firms) are perfect agents of shareholders in the sense that the managers seek to maximize the stock price and thereby maximize the shareholders' wealth. In the following section, we relax this assumption.

5.1.1   Divergence of stockholder and bondholder interests[1]

Stockholders' and bondholders' interests regularly diverge for several reasons, here we will focus on the *Dividend Payout Problem*, the *Claim*

Dilution Problem, the *Asset Substitution Problem*, and the *Underinvestment Problem*.

The Dividend Payout Problem. If a firm were to issue bonds that were priced based on the assumption that the firm would maintain its current payout policy (both dividends and share repurchases), the value of the bonds would be reduced by increasing payouts financed either through asset liquidations or out of internally generated funds. For example, in the limit, if the firm were to sell all its assets and pay a liquidating dividend to shareholders, the bondholders would be left with worthless claims, while the stockholders would capture the full value of all the firm's assets.

As we discussed in Chapter 3, equity claims in a simple levered firm can be viewed as call options: stockholders have the option to purchase the firm's assets from the bondholders at an exercise price equal to the face value of the firm's (zero-coupon) bonds. If a dividend is paid, financed either by liquidating assets or using internally generated funds, the value of the firm's assets would fall by the amount of the dividend. The value of the stock, however, falls by less than the value of the dividend (the equity's delta, the change in the stock price from a change in the value of the underlying assets, is less than one). Thus, wealth is transferred from the bondholders to the stockholders – the shareholders receive the full value of the dividend, which exceeds the drop in the share price. For example, if the delta is .5, a $10 dividend paid to shareholders would reduce the share price by $5. This Dividend Payout Problem is less significant in the typical case when the value of the firm's assets is well in excess of the face value of the bonds (delta approaches one as the stockholders' option moves deep in the money).

The Claim Dilution Problem. If the firm were to sell bonds that were priced based on the assumption that no additional debt would be issued, the value of the existing bondholders' claims would be reduced by issuing additional debt of the same – or higher – priority and using the proceeds of the bond issue to repurchase shares. This reduction in the value of the bonds would be captured by the stockholders.

Issuing additional claims of the same priority and maturity increases the probability of default and thus lowers the value of any currently outstanding bonds. If the proceeds of the new bond issue were used to repurchase a portion of the firm's stock, there would be a wealth transfer from the old bondholders to the shareholders. And if the new bonds were of a higher priority or had a shorter time to maturity, the reduction in the value of the old bonds – and thus the wealth transfer from bondholders to stockholders – would be greater.

The Asset Substitution Problem. If the firm were to sell bonds to bondholders who expected that the firm would undertake low volatility projects, the bonds would be priced accordingly. But the value of the stockholders' equity rises, and the value of the bondholders' claims falls, if the firm were to substitute projects that increased the volatility of the firm's assets. (The higher volatility increases the value of the stockholders' option on the firm's assets, but the value of the bonds falls because of the higher default risk.)

The simple exchange of high-risk assets for low-risk assets has no effect on firm value if both have the same NPV. However, shareholders can have incentives to invest in projects with negative NPVs if the increase in the volatility of the firm's assets from undertaking these projects is sufficiently large. Even though such projects would reduce the total value of the firm, the value of the equity would rise. By engaging in risky projects that increase the volatility of the firm's asset value, the value of the option-like payoff that the shareholders have on the firm increases, while the price of the bonds falls because of the higher default risk. For the sake of illustration, consider the following extreme example: Suppose the firm has no positive NPV projects. Its sole asset is $100 in cash that is just sufficient to meet its obligations to the bondholders in one year. In this case, the equity would be worthless, since there is no chance of the stockholders receiving a future payoff. From the stockholders' perspective, it would be better to take a "wild gamble" and invest the $100 in a negative NPV project so long as the volatility of the project were great enough. At least under some circumstances, the project might pay off more than $100 so that the firm might pay off its bondholders and still have something left for its stockholders. Incentives to engage in such behavior are particularly high if the firm is in financial distress; the stockholders have little to lose if the risky gamble does not pay off. In this case, the cost is borne by the firm's bondholders – not its shareholders.

The Underinvestment Problem. Myers (1977) argues that a substantial portion of the value of firms often is composed of intangible assets in the form of future investment opportunities. A firm with bonds outstanding can have incentives to reject a positive NPV project if the benefits from accepting the project primarily accrue to the bondholders. For example, suppose that a firm has an obligation to pay its bondholders $100 in one year. With no new investment, default by the firm on its bonds is likely. If so, the bondholders will assume title to the assets of the firm, which will be valued at something less than $100. Suppose that the firm has a positive NPV project that is expected to allow the firm to meet its obligation to its bondholders – but with little additional value left for the shareholders. It would be irrational for the shareholders to contribute capital to fund this project; the bondholders capture enough of the benefits that what would be left for the stockholders would fail to provide a normal rate of return on the capital contributed. More generally, if the value of the option that the shareholders have on the firm's assets increases by less than the cost of the project, then this firm's stockholders have no financial incentive to fund the project.

This Underinvestment Problem is most severe when the firm's asset value is low compared to the face value of the bonds, especially if the maturity date of the bonds is near. But in the normal case where the value of the firm's assets greatly exceeds the face value of the bonds, the stockholders capture almost all of the value created by investing in a positive NPV project.

5.1.2   Bondholder-stockholder conflicts: agency costs

Rational bondholders recognize these potential conflicts of interest and understand that shareholders have the potential to take actions that would increase their wealth at the bondholders' expense. In pricing a bond issue, bondholders are expected to forecast the likely behavior of the stockholders, given the investment, financing, and payout policies that are available to them. The price that bondholders are willing to pay for an issue will be lower to reflect the likelihood of subsequent wealth transfers to stockholders. This price adjustment allows bondholders to earn the market-determined expected rate of return on their investment. Any reduction in firm value that occurs due to these incentive conflicts (for example, from foregoing positive NPV projects) will therefore be borne ultimately by the firm's stockholders.

In the sort of perfect capital market imagined by M&M, these agency conflicts would be controlled costlessly by appropriate contractual agreements. However, in the actual markets within which firms must operate, contracting costs and asymmetric information generally will make it impossible to resolve these conflicts at no cost. Although covenants included in bond contracts can be used to help control these problems (for example, covenants that restrict payouts to shareholders), these contractual provisions do not control these problems completely. Appropriately designed covenants, however, can reduce the opportunity cost (the residual loss), which results when the shareholders of a levered firm follow a policy that does not maximize firm value. And if a covenant lowers the costs that bondholders incur in monitoring shareholders, the price they are willing to pay for the bonds increases. Thus, the cost-reducing benefits of such a covenant also are captured by the firm's stockholders.

Agency costs of debt include the cost of writing, monitoring, bonding, and enforcing debt contracts as well as the residual loss from incomplete control of these incentive problems. Although these costs could be avoided by issuing no debt, there are potentially important offsetting benefits of including debt in the firm's capital structure, benefits that are in addition to the tax-related benefits discussed in Chapter 4.

5.2   Stockholder-manager conflicts

Corporate shareholders typically delegate most strategic and operating decisions to professional managers. Senior executives, in turn, delegate many decisions to lower-level managers (as well as other employees throughout the firm). Economic theory characterizes individuals as creative maximizers of their own utility. Thus, the collection of individuals that comprise the firm are unlikely to have incentives that are automatically aligned. Corporate stockholders, who own title to the firm's residual cash flows (what is left after other of the firm's claimants are paid), are likely to be interested in maximizing the present value of these cash flows. Senior executives, as well as other agents within the firm, do not share this goal necessarily.

In our earlier discussions, we have assumed that decisions are made within a firm to maximize its value. But professional managers, who are granted the authority to make most strategic and operating decisions, have only a limited equity investment in their firms and, consequently, can have other objectives. To understand corporate financial decisions better, it is important to take a closer look at the potential agency conflicts between shareholders and managers – particularly the firm's Chief Executive Officer (CEO).

5.2.1   Divergence of manager and stockholder interests[2]

As in our discussion of stockholder-bondholder conflicts, we begin by assuming a quite simple contract: Suppose a potential CEO is offered a contract that specifies a starting salary and a fixed raise each year until mandatory retirement at age 65. The CEO may quit at any time (perhaps to take a better job), but the firm can dismiss the CEO earlier only if the firm files for bankruptcy. In this case, there are at least five potential sources of conflict that can arise between stockholders and this manager. Particularly important for our purposes are the *Effort Problem*, the *Perquisite Consumption Problem*, the *Differential Risk Exposure Problem*, the *Differential Horizon Problem*, and the *Free Cash Flow Problem*.

The Effort Problem. Additional effort by managers generally increases firm value, but since managers expend the effort, this additional effort reduces their well-being.

The Perquisite Consumption Problem. It is in the interests of shareholders to pay sufficient salaries to attract and retain competent managers; however, stockholders do not want to over-compensate them. In contrast, managers are likely to want not only higher salaries but also firm-provided perquisites such as generous expense budgets, use of a luxurious automobile and a corporate jet, exclusive club memberships, and lavish office furniture.

The Differential Risk Exposure Problem. Stockholders generally include their shares in a well-diversified portfolio. This implies that stockholders should be most concerned with the stock's systematic risk (beta); they can handle the idiosyncratic risk effectively and economically through diversification. But managers typically have much of their human capital as well as their personal financial wealth invested in the firm. Managers have only one career; they understandably worry about the firm's total risk.[3]

The Differential Horizons Problem. Managers' claims on the firm generally are limited by their tenure with the firm, and thus managers can have limited incentives to care about cash flows that extend beyond their tenure. But stockholders are interested in the value of the entire future stream of cash flows, since that is what determines the price at which they can sell their shares.

The Free Cash Flow (Overinvestment) Problem. Jensen (1986) defines *free cash flow* as cash flow generated by the firm in excess of that required to fund available positive NPV projects. Corporate executives can have incentives to invest in negative NPV projects. For example, they might be reluctant to reduce the size of the firm, even if all available positive NPV projects have been exhausted. By retaining funds within the firm and investing them in a negative NPV project, there is a larger buffer to avoid bankruptcy and job loss. Also, an executive understandably might be reluctant to dismiss colleagues and friends in a no-longer-profitable division – the executive bears most of the costs (disutility) while stock-holders receive most of the benefits. Executives might gain more prestige and compensation from running a larger firm.

Below we focus on how these agency-related conflicts potentially affect a firm's capital structure. In Chapter 8, we extend this discussion to include corporate payout policy. For a more general summary of the research on other corporate governance mechanisms that help to control agency conflicts with a firm (for example, executive compensation and monitoring by the board of directors), see Hermalin and Weisbach (2017).

5.2.2   Using debt to control the free cash flow and other agency problems

One potential benefit of debt financing is that it allows managers to make a more credible promise to pay out, rather than retain, future free cash flow (Jensen, 1986). If managers fail to make specified interest and principal payments, the firm can be forced into bankruptcy, something managers obviously would like to avoid. (Note that executive turnover increases substantially when a firm files for bankruptcy.) The greater threat of failure also can be important in motivating managers to exert effort to increase firm productivity and efficiency and in so doing mitigate the Effort Problem.

Especially within firms whose value primarily reflects that of its tangible assets, more cash is frequently generated than can be reinvested within the firm productively. In such circumstances, some managers are inclined to use this free cash flow to sustain growth at the expense of profitability, either through misguided efforts to gain market share within a mature business or through diversifying acquisitions.[4] To maximize firm value, such managers must distribute free cash flow to investors; raising leverage may add value by improving managers' incentives to do so.

Substituting debt for equity at the direction of the company's Board of Directors (perhaps in the form of a leveraged share repurchase) is likely to be an effective means of addressing this Free Cash Flow Problem. Contractually obligated payments of interest and principal are quite effective ways of committing managers to distribute free cash flow to investors, both now and into the future – more effective than discretionary dividends or share repurchases. And within industries generating substantial cash flow but facing few growth opportunities (think of the tobacco industry today), debt financing can have the beneficial effect of causing managers otherwise inclined to overinvest to be more critical in evaluating capital spending plans.

In mature industries with limited capital requirements, higher leverage also facilitates equity ownership concentration. Concentration of ownership in turn allows for more effective monitoring of corporate managers by active investors like Warren Buffett; Kohlberg, Kravis and Roberts (KKR), and Forstmann Little, which can help to control all of the above-mentioned agency conflicts.

5.3   Underinvestment and free cash flow – implications for target leverage

Firms vary substantially in their investment opportunity sets. Growth firms have numerous positive NPV projects in which to invest. Other firms have few, deriving most of their value from what Stew Myers calls "assets in place." Since the potential problems associated with underinvestment and free cash flow depend on the firm's investment opportunities, the optimal leverage ratio of a firm (holding other factors constant) is likely to depend on whether firm value primarily reflects the value of its growth options or its assets in place. Table 5.1 summarizes these theoretical and empirical implications. The table summarizes how the costs of debt associated with the Underinvestment Problem and the benefits of debt associated with the Free Cash Flow (Overinvestment) Problem vary with the firm's investment opportunity set (assets in place versus growth opportunities). The predicted effect on leverage is shown.

Table 5.1   Investment opportunities, contracting costs, and leverage choices

	Investment opportunity set spectrum	
	Assets in place	Growth options
	←	→
Underinvestment costs of debt	Low	High
Free cash-flow benefits of debt	High	Low
Predicted leverage	High	Low

This table summarizes how the costs of debt associated with the Underinvestment Problem and the benefits of debt associated with the Free Cash Flow (Overinvestment) Problem vary with the firm's investment opportunity set (assets in place versus growth opportunities). The predicted effect on leverage is shown.

Assets in Place Firms. On the one hand, for firms whose value primarily reflects the expected cash flows from long-lived tangible assets, benefits from controlling the Underinvestment Problem are small. For a firm with few profitable growth options, the temptation to underinvest that is accentuated by high leverage is unlikely to be very costly – they simply have few profitable investment opportunities from which they might walk away. However, the benefits of leverage in controlling the Free Cash Flow Problem are likely to be quite large. With lots of internally generated cash, management within these firms can face great temptations to retain funds far beyond their ability to profitably deploy them. Setting a high leverage target (by the firm's Board of Directors) can be a way of making a credible promise to investors that these funds will be distributed rather than retained.

Growth Firms. On the other hand, for firms whose value primarily consists of growth opportunities, the costs associated with failing to exercise valuable growth options can be quite large. Thus, for these firms, the Underinvestment Problem should be of great concern. Firms with substantial growth options frequently have little internally generated cash yet face ample opportunities to profitably reinvest any funds – in this case, free cash flow is negative. The benefits of debt in controlling the incentive to overinvest are insignificant. With few benefits but high costs of leverage, the theory predicts that such firms will have low leverage targets.

5.4   Capital structure implications of asymmetric information

Thus far in this chapter we have focused on how agency conflicts among stockholders, managers, and bondholders can affect a firm's capital structure. Another set of capital structure models, to which we now turn, focus more generally on how asymmetric information between managers and current as well as potential stockholders can affect financing decisions.

Incentive conflicts between stockholders and managers would be easier to control if all participants in the market had low-cost access to the same set of information. Senior corporate executives, however, invariably have better information about the value of their firms than current or potential outside investors – information is asymmetric. After all, corporate executives spend much of their time analyzing the firm's products, markets, strategies, and investment opportunities. Executives also have more timely information about current operating performance and better access to firm-specific information useful in forecasting short-run earnings.

Thus, it is not surprising that researchers have found that corporate officers tend to earn higher than average returns when they buy or sell their own company's stock (Seyhun, 1986). Nor is it surprising that the stock market reacts when managers announce major corporate decisions. For example, if a company announces a change in its capital expenditures or research and development expenses, investors will draw some inference about the profitability of the firm's investment opportunities from this announcement and adjust its stock price accordingly (Smith, 1986a).

5.4.1 Signaling and capital structure

With better information about the value of their firms than outside investors, managers are likely to face circumstances where they would like to communicate positive information to the market. Unfortunately, this task might not be as easy as it sounds. Since virtually all managers would like their stock prices to be higher than they are currently, simply announcing that their firms are undervalued is unlikely to be convincing. Thus, managers who wish to communicate positive news to the market must identify a credible mechanism to convey this information. As Nobel laureate Michael Spence (1973) points out, information disclosed by an obviously biased source (management, in this case) will be credible only if the costs of communicating falsely are large enough to induce managers to reveal information truthfully. Although there are several potentially effective signaling devices available to managers, a change in leverage is a noteworthy candidate.

Debt and equity differ in several ways that are important for signaling purposes. First, debt contracts oblige the firm to make a fixed set of cash payments over the life of the contract. If these payments are not made, there are serious consequences – potentially including bankruptcy. Equity, however, is more forgiving. Although stockholders typically expect dividend payments to be maintained from year to year, if not actually increased, managers have more discretion over these payments and can choose to cut – or even omit – them in times of financial distress.

For this reason, adding more debt to the firm's capital structure might serve as a credible signal of high expected future cash flows. By committing the firm to make future interest payments and principal repayments to bondholders, managers might communicate their confidence that the firm will have sufficient cash flows to meet these future obligations. Moreover, the costs of false signaling are high. If future cash flows are insufficient to meet their obligated payments to bondholders, the firm can be forced into bankruptcy – an event frequently associated with senior executives losing their jobs.

Ross's Signaling Model. Ross (1977) presents a formal signaling model in which higher leverage allows "high-quality" firms to distinguish themselves from "low-quality" firms to outside investors. In this model, managers of high-quality firms consciously want to convey positive information to outsiders and choose higher leverage to do so. In the *separating* *equilibrium* (where high-quality firms are able to separate themselves from low-quality firms), managers of firms without positive information refrain from copying this signal, since higher leverage would increase the likelihood of their firms becoming financially distressed.

We think that three points are important to make about Ross's and other formal signaling models. First, we believe that it is important to distinguish these models from a more basic informational asymmetry. With an informational asymmetry a potential investor, in thinking about the manager's information set, would reason: *I know that you know more than I know.* Signaling models take that reasoning a step further. They presume that managers, in considering the information set of potential investors would reason: *I know that you know that I know more than you know* – and here is the critical part – *and I am going to choose actions specifically designed to manage your expectations.* Few scholars doubt the informational asymmetry; but there is a serious debate about the managerial importance of this last convolution required by signaling models. Second, signaling models typically are derived within a single-period framework. But within a multi-period setting, a policy of signaling employing leverage whenever management has positive private information potentially creates a problem when management does not provide that signal. In that case, investors quite reasonably might wonder: *What negative information might management have that they are not disclosing?* Third, Ross's signaling theory perhaps has more to say about corporate financing policy – the choice of debt or equity when raising external capital – than about a company's leverage target.

5.4.2   Pecking order theory

The information costs associated with debt and equity issues led Myers and Majluf (1984) to argue that a company's capital structure simply reflects the accumulation of their past financing requirements, and that leverage ratios change largely in response to imbalances between internally generated cash flows and investment opportunities. According to this argument – which they call the *Pecking Order* – a company will finance new investments with the "cheapest available" source of funds. Specifically, it employs internally generated funds (retained earnings) first. If internal funds are insufficient, it will employ debt next because of its lower flotation and information costs.[5] Within this model, a company issues equity only as a last resort – only when its debt capacity has been exhausted.

The Pecking Order Theory suggests that companies with fewer investment opportunities and substantial free cash flow will have lower leverage, and that higher-growth firms with lower operating cash flows will have higher leverage. In short, the Pecking Order Model produces a set of predictions that are precisely the opposite of those offered by the contracting cost and tax arguments that we discussed above.

5.4.3   Mispriced securities and market timing

As we discussed in Chapter 3, debt and equity claims differ with respect to their sensitivity to changes in firm value. Because the promised payments to bondholders are fixed, stock prices are more sensitive to changes in firm value than bond prices. Consider the plight of a CFO who wishes to raise additional capital by selling debt or equity, but who believes that both securities are currently undervalued. Now if this undervaluation is sufficiently large, the CFO might choose to forgo a security issue altogether.

But if the decision is to proceed, a CFO intent on preserving value would choose to sell the security that is less undervalued. In this case, the choice would be to issue debt because debt is less sensitive to mispricing than equity. Alternatively, if the firm were overvalued, this CFO would be more likely to choose to issue the more overvalued security – in this case, equity.

Similar logic leads Baker and Wurgler (2002) to suggest that managers regularly take advantage of their superior information and have equity offers only when their stock is substantially overpriced. Similar to the Pecking Order Theory, they suggest that firms do not have a target leverage around which they manage, rather the observed level of leverage is simply the accumulation of the combination of past attempts to raise external capital on the most attractive terms available plus the firm's ability to generate cash from internal operations. Asserting that the substantial increase in stock prices that regularly precedes offerings is evidence of mispricing, they argue that their Market Timing Model explains why equity offers are rare – much less frequent than debt offers – why there is a substantial increase in the stock price preceding an equity offering, as well as why the stock price typically falls at the announcement of an equity offer.

They assume that, just as in the case of insider trading, managers have an informational advantage that provides an opportunity to sell overvalued shares to less-informed investors. But we should note that their argument ignores a profound difference between insider trades and equity offerings. Insider trades are announced only after the transaction; equity offerings are announced before. As Nobel laureate George Akerlof (1970) maintains, this prior announcement effectively undermines their assumed method of profiting from their informational advantage – it puts potential investors "on notice" that senior corporate executives think that their share price is too high. If, as Baker and Wurgler assume, this were the only reason a firm would have an equity offering, it would cause a reduction in the price investors are willing to pay for the shares – both existing shares and the to-be-newly issued shares. This predictable price adjustment would mean that managers would have to increase the amount of "over-pricing" that they require to trigger an equity offer. But that would lead to an even bigger price adjustment at announcement. Ultimately, observed equity offerings would only be by firms with the largest level of overpricing; such a market would effectively collapse.

5.5   Summary

In this chapter, we begin by discussing four potential conflicts of interest between bondholders and stockholders: the Dividend Payout Problem, the Asset Substitution Problem, the Claim Dilution Problem, and the Underinvestment Problem. Controlling these conflicts entails both out-of-pocket costs (monitoring and bonding costs) as well as the opportunity cost of incomplete control of these conflicts (the residual loss). These agency costs generally increase with the amount of debt in the firm's capital structure and should be considered in selecting a leverage target. These costs are likely to be highest in firms that face a reasonable likelihood of defaulting on their bonds and have positive NPV growth opportunities.

We then consider potential conflicts between stockholders and managers. We discuss five potential conflicts: The Effort Problem, the Perquisite

Consumption Problem, the Differential Risk Exposure Problem, the Differential Horizons Problem, and the Free Cash Flow (Overinvestment) Problem. Managers might prefer to retain free cash flow (cash flow in excess of that necessary to fund available positive NPV projects), rather than distribute it to the firm's stockholders. A potential benefit of debt in the firm's capital structure is that it commits the managers to make payouts to the firm's investors. This benefit is likely to be greatest among firms with significant cash inflows from existing corporate assets but limited new investment opportunities. Debt obligations also can motivate managers to exert additional effort to avoid financial distress. In addition, in mature industries with limited capital requirements, higher leverage facilitates equity ownership concentration, which can promote more effective monitoring of managers by shareholders.

The Tradeoff Theory argues that firms have target leverage ratios that reflect a tradeoff between their incremental benefits and costs of debt. A combined analysis of the Underinvestment and Free Cash Flow (Overinvestment) Problems suggests that firms consisting primarily of assets in place will have higher leverage than growth firms (holding other factors constant).

After discussing agency conflicts among stockholders, bondholders, and managers, we turn our attention to issues of Information Asymmetry. Managers often possess information about the true values of their firms that is superior to that of external investors. The Signaling, Pecking Order, and Market Timing models each are based on aspects of this informational asymmetry.

Notes

1. This section draws on discussions in Smith and Warner (1979).
2. This section draws on discussions in Smith and Watts (1982).
3. In various academic papers where this issue is discussed, owners and managers are assumed to have different utility functions; shareholders are risk neutral and managers are risk averse. We argue that it is not their preferences that differ, but their opportunities to manage risk that are important.
4. Diversification reduces the volatility of a firm's cash flows, but this by itself does not affect firm value, since shareholders can diversify on their own account by selecting appropriate investment portfolios. Diversifying acquisitions often reduce the combined value of firms, since the acquiring firm's

management may not be well suited for managing the combined entity. Diversification is most likely to increase value when there are economies of scope or scale that produce higher cash flows by combining the two firms.

5.   Potential investors recognize that managers are likely to have superior information. Thus, when the firm's managers announce a planned transaction, such as the sale of new shares, potential investors "price protect" themselves against the possibility that managers are attempting to take advantage of their superior information (that is, they will be willing to purchase the new securities only at a discount). This "information cost" is likely to be lower for debt than equity since its value is less sensitive to estimates of firm value.

6   Determinants of leverage: the evidence

Up to this point, we have discussed various theories of how firms choose their capital structures, or more precisely what factors are likely to be important in this choice. Although there currently is no comprehensive theory to explain exactly how firms choose their capital structures, the existing theories have the potential to provide managers with an array of useful insights. A fundamental empirical question is which, if any, of these theories helps to explain observed capital structure choices?

At the most general level, there are at least two primary theories on how firms choose their capital structures: The *Tradeoff Theory* and the *Pecking Order Theory* (Myers, 1984 and Frank and Goyal, 2008). The Tradeoff Theory primarily focuses on the firm's economic balance sheet and argues there are costs and benefits to debt financing.[1] The potential costs of debt come from the direct and indirect costs of financial distress, including the Underinvestment Problem. The potential benefits of debt come from corporate tax savings and mitigation of the Free Cash-Flow (Overinvestment) Problem. According to the Tradeoff Theory, depending on such things as the firm's tax circumstances and investment opportunity set, there is an optimal target capital structure that the firm adjusts toward over time.[2]

In contrast, the Pecking Order Theory primarily focuses on the firm's economic cash flow statement and argues that firms do not have well-defined target leverage ratios – at least among its more extreme forms. According to the Pecking Order Theory, managers have a strict preference for internal over external financing and, when the firm must raise funds externally, debt over equity financing.[3] Observed capital structures are simply the accumulated result of past investment requirements and financing opportunities.

An important empirical question is which, if either, of these general theories is better at explaining observed capital structure choices? Another important question is if managers actually trade off the benefits and costs of debt to determine a target capital structure, which of the suggested costs and benefits are most important?

In the late 1970s and early 1980s, finance researchers began to conduct empirical tests of alternative theories of capital structure. Since then, numerous researchers have provided additional evidence on this topic. In this chapter, we summarize the evidence from capital structure studies and discuss what inferences and insights can be drawn from it. While our primary focus is on the Tradeoff and Pecking Order Theories, we also provide brief discussions of the evidence on the market timing, signaling, and behavioral explanations of capital structure choices.

6.1   Empirical studies in corporate finance – some limitations

Before examining the evidence, we should acknowledge that empirical research in corporate finance has lagged behind that in capital markets. We believe that there are several reasons for this.

First, the models in corporate finance are less precise than asset pricing models. Models of capital structure typically provide only "qualitative" or directional predictions. For example, models that emphasize tax considerations predict that companies with more non-interest tax shields (like foreign tax credits) will have less debt in their capital structures – but the theory does not tell us how much less.

Second, most of the theoretical arguments are not mutually exclusive. Evidence consistent with one explanation (for example, that taxes are important) does not allow us to conclude that another factor (say, the role of debt in controlling overinvestment by mature companies) is unimportant. In fact, it is likely that taxes, financial distress costs (including underinvestment), and information costs all play some role in determining various aspects of a firm's financial policies. Critically, this means that if growth options, for example, have impacts on leverage choices both under the Tradeoff Theory and under the Pecking Order Theory, the estimated coefficient will reflect the algebraic sum of the two effects. Thus, in estimating a reduced form regression, a coefficient might be insignificant either because: (1) the variable is unimportant in corporate leverage decisions or (2) there are two effects, both similarly important, but with offsetting signs. And with two potential effects, a significant coefficient should be interpreted as one has a larger impact on leverage choices than the other – not that one is important and the other is unimportant.

Third, to sort out the various impacts that an independent variable might have in the corporate leverage decision would require a well-specified structural model, not just a reduced form regression. But given our current state of knowledge, getting a structural model identified is difficult. Variables important in the corporate leverage decision also frequently are important in payout policy decisions (as well as other aspects of the firm's financial policy like debt maturity, priority structure, use of convertibility provisions, etc.).

Fourth, many of the variables that researchers think should affect a firm's target capital structure are difficult to measure. For example, tax explanations argue that the firm's marginal tax rate is important, but corporate tax returns are confidential; a firm's marginal tax rate (as well as other details of a firm's tax return) cannot be directly observed by outside researchers.

For these reasons (as well as others), the state of the art in empirical verification within corporate finance is less developed than in asset pricing. Nonetheless, there has been considerable progress. Although we may never be able to pinpoint with certainty a firm's value-maximizing capital structure, we have learned a great deal about the nature of the tradeoffs between debt and equity – tradeoffs that every CFO should consider in making financing decisions.

6.2   Evidence from panel studies[4]

6.2.1   Empirical design

A relatively large number of studies provide evidence on capital structure based on panel datasets – datasets that include annual observations for a large sample of firms typically over a period of several decades.[5] Many studies limit the analysis to unregulated firms (excluding firms from the financial, utility, and railroad industries), but others include them in their analyses.

The typical study estimates regression models in which the dependent variable is the leverage ratio for a given firm in a given year. Explanatory variables include proxies for hard-to-observe variables suggested by the various theories (for example, the firm's marginal tax rate and the expected costs of financial distress) and possible control variables, such as year and firm-level fixed effects. Theories are tested by examining the signs and significance levels of the estimated coefficients for the explanatory variables of interest.

Although some studies focus on *book leverage* (the book value of debt divided by the sum of the book value of debt plus the book value of equity), other studies focus on *market leverage* – typically proxied by the book value of debt divided by the sum of the book value of assets minus the book value of equity plus the market value of equity (market equity plus the book value of the non-equity liability-side claims). The book value of debt is used in the calculation of market leverage because virtually all firms have bank and other non-public debt, and some firms have no public debt at all; thus, the market value of debt typically is unobservable. We believe that capital structure and financing policy decisions are economic decisions, so in this chapter our primary focus is on results using market leverage. We begin by summarizing the collective evidence and then turn to interpreting it within the context of the Tradeoff versus Pecking Order Theories.

6.2.2 Significant factors

Researchers have included numerous explanatory variables in their regression models. Many of these variables have proven to be either insignificant or not consistently significant across studies and specifications. Studies have found four factors to be consistently and significantly associated with leverage. Firms with high market-to-book ratios (market value of equity plus the book value of debt divided by the book value of total assets) typically have lower leverage ratios. Large firms and those with more tangible assets typically have higher leverage. Leverage generally falls with the firm's profitability.[6]

Researchers have included various proxies for the firm's marginal tax rate (for example, whether the firm has investment tax credits or tax-loss carryforwards). It is fair to conclude that there is no consistent evidence that leverage ratios are associated with these tax proxies.[7]

Table 6.1, derived from Graham, Leary and Roberts (2015), is representative of the results found in panel studies of capital structure. Their results are based on a large sample consisting of all nonfinancial and unregulated firms in any given year that are listed on CRSP and either COMPUSTAT or Moody's. The estimated models include firm-level fixed effects, which control for factors that affect an individual firm's capital structure and are constant over time. To facilitate comparison of magnitudes, the estimated coefficients have been multiplied by the standard deviation of each independent variable within each decade. The table shows that the four above-mentioned variables are consistently significant in explaining market leverage ratios. In all of the decades from the 1920s through the 2010s, market leverage is positively associated with firm size and tangible assets and negatively associated with the market-to-book ratio and profitability. The estimated models explain from 9% to 30% (adjusted R^2) of the variation in capital structures across the decades.[8] The estimated coefficients are not only statistically significant but also relatively large in magnitude. A one standard deviation change in any of the explanatory variables in the most recent decade implies a change in the firm's market leverage by around four to six percentage points (relative to a mean leverage ratio of around 25%). Lemmon, Roberts and Zender (2008), however, find that the estimated coefficients in leverage regressions, although generally significant and of the same sign, vary substantially depending on the specification. Thus, evidence on the magnitude of the effects should be interpreted with some caution.

Table 6.2 from Rajan and Zingales (1995) shows that these four key variables explain about the same proportion of the variation in capital structures in Japan, Germany, France, the United Kingdom, and Canada, as they do in the United States. Moreover, the signs and significance levels of the coefficients generally are similar across countries. Growth opportunities, as measured by market-to-book, is negative and significant in all seven countries. In a few cases, tangible assets, firm size, and profitability are insignificant in selected countries. Oztekin (2015) extends the analysis to 35 countries and finds firm size, tangibility, and profitability to be reliable determinants of capital structures throughout the world. Consistent with some other studies, he also finds that leverage is positively related to expected inflation and overall industry leverage.

Table 6.1   The association between market leverage and growth opportunities, firm size, tangible assets, and profitability by decade from 1925–2010

	Growth Opportunities	Firm Size	Tangible Assets	Profitability	ADJ R-squared
1925–30	-1.83***	12.36***	82.39	-5.99***	0.15
1931–40	-2.57***	0.42	5.67***	-3.64***	0.09
1941–50	-3.40***	6.91***	3.25***	-4.10***	0.11
1951–60	-4.24***	4.30***	1.16	-4.72***	0.15
1961–70	-4.51***	13.97***	1.39**	-6.06***	0.3
1971–80	-6.41***	10.05***	3.99***	-6.98***	0.23
1981–90	-6.29***	11.94***	4.10***	-5.83***	0.19
1991–00	-4.64***	11.14***	3.62***	-5.00***	0.16
2001–10	-4.33***	6.06***	5.51***	-3.85***	0.11

This table displays the results from regressions of market leverage on measures of growth opportunities, firm size, tangible assets, and profitability by decade. The sample includes all firms in the CRSP database that are also covered either in COMPUSTAT or Moody's Manuals. Financial firms, utilities, and railroads are excluded from the analysis. Firm-level fixed effects are included as controls. To facilitate comparison of magnitudes, the estimated coefficients have been multiplied by the standard deviation of each independent variable within each decade. Growth opportunities are measured by the firm's market-to-book ratio; firm size is measure by the log of real sales; tangible assets are measured by net plant, property, and equipment divided by total assets; profitability is measured by earnings before interest and taxes divided by total assets.
Note: *** Significant at the .01 level.
Source: This table presents a subset of the results reported in Table 2 of Graham, Leary and Roberts (2015).

Table 6.2   The association between market leverage and tangibility of assets, growth opportunities, firm size, and profitability by country

	US	Japan	Germany	France	Italy	UK	Canada
Tangible Assets	0.33***	0.58***	0.28*	0.18	0.48**	0.27***	0.11
Growth Opportunities	-0.08***	-0.07***	-0.21***	-0.15**	-0.18*	-0.06**	-0.13***
Firm Size	0.03***	0.07***	-0.06***	-0.00	0.04	0.01	0.05***
Profitability	-0.6***	-2.25***	0.17	-0.22	-0.95	-0.47**	-0.48***
# of observations	2207	313	176	126	98	544	275
Pseudo R-squared	0.19		0.14	0.28	0.12	0.19	0.3

This table displays the results from regressions of market leverage in 1991 on measures of asset tangibility, growth opportunities, firm size, and profitability for seven countries. Financial firms are excluded from the analysis Tangible assets are measured by the ratio of fixed assets to total assets; Growth opportunities are measured by the firm's market-to-book ratio; firm size is measure by the log of real sales; profitability is measured by earnings before interest, taxes, depreciation, and amortization divided by total assets. All the explanatory variables are four-year averages (1987–1990). Most of the underlying data came from Global Vantage, which maintained a large database on stock prices and accounting data for many international companies.
*Note: * , ** , and ***, significant at the 10, 5, and 1 percent level, respectively.*
Source: This table presents a subset of the results reported in Table IX of Rajan and Zingales (1995).

6.3   Interpreting the results

So, what do these findings tell us about the validity of the alternative theories? Table 6.3 summarizes the five underlying variables of interest, commonly used proxies for them, the predicted leverage associations from the Tradeoff and Pecking Order Theories, and the signs of the estimated leverage associations. Before discussing specific variables, we should note that while the more extreme versions of the Pecking Order Theory argue that firms do not have target leverage ratios, they still suggest associations between leverage and various variables of interest (for example, holding other factors constant, more profitable firms are likely to have lower leverage because they will tend to have higher levels of internally generated cash). Below, we discuss in more detail how the existing findings can be interpreted in relation to the two primary theories.[9]

Table 6.3   Variables of interest, common proxies, predicted effects on leverage, and the empirical findings

Variable of Interest	Common Proxy Variable	Tradeoff Theory Prediction	Pecking Order Prediction	Documented Association with Market Leverage
Corporate Marginal Tax Rate	Existence of Investment Tax Shields or Tax-Loss Carry Forwards	Positive Assosciation	No Assocaition	No Association
Growth Opportunities	Market-to-Book Ratio	Negative Association	Positive Association	Negative Association
Firm Size	Sales or Total Asssets	Positive Assosciation	Negative or No Association	Positive Association
Tangible Assets	Plant, Property & Equipment Scaled by Total Assets	Positive Assosciation	Negative or No Association	Positive Association
Profitablity	EBIT/Total Assets	Positive Assosciation	Negative Association	Negative Association

This table lists corporate taxes and four underlying variables and their proxies that have been found to be consistently significant in empirical studies of capital structure. The predicted association with leverage from the Tradeoff and Pecking Order theories are provided, along with the signs of the association documented in existing empirical studies.

6.3.1   Leverage and corporate tax rates

Early tradeoff models argue that the primary benefit of debt is lower corporate taxes. The Pecking Order Theory argues that taxes are not an important consideration when it comes to raising capital. All firms are predicted to have the same ordering of financing preferences – internally generated funds, debt, and equity only as a last resort. The empirical results suggest that taxes are not a reliably important consideration in leverage decisions (at least for the typical firm). However, the power of these tests may be low: (1) There are challenges in identifying a firm's current marginal tax rate because of data limitations. Financial accounting and tax accounting, although clearly related, are different. For instance, the value of an interest tax shield depends on taxable income, but financial academics only have data from GAAP accounting statements. (2) Most corporate debt has a multi-year duration; its current marginal tax rate may be a poor proxy for expected tax circumstances over the life of the debt instrument. (3) Much of the debt outstanding today was issued earlier, when the firm potentially faced quite different tax circumstances. (4) It is possible that there are two offsetting tax effects, both important, but difficult to disentangle employing standard statistical methods. Nonetheless, these findings tend to support the Pecking Order Theory and suggest that if the Tradeoff Theory is valid, the primary benefits from issuing debt likely come from some other source than tax savings (for example, controlling the Overinvestment Problem).

6.3.2   Leverage and the firm's investment opportunity set

Researchers commonly use the market-to-book ratio as a proxy for growth opportunities within the firm's investment opportunity set. Growth firms generally have relatively high market-to-book ratios, since investment opportunities should be reflected in market prices but not accounting statements, which focus on historical book values. The documented negative relation between leverage and the market-to-book ratio is consistent with the Tradeoff Theory, especially versions that emphasize agency-related costs and benefits of debt (for example, see Barclay and Smith, 2005).

The Tradeoff Theory predicts a negative association between leverage and growth opportunities for at least two reasons. First, the indirect costs of financial distress are likely to be higher for growth firms. Of particular concern here is the Underinvestment Problem, which arises when managers of levered firms shun positive NPV projects because much of the gains go to bondholders, not stockholders. This problem is more important in growth firms since they face a broader array of positive NPV projects in which to invest and are likely to lose more value if they were to become financially distressed. This problem is less important in asset-intensive (value) firms facing more limited investment opportunities. Second is the Overinvestment Problem. It arises when managers have incentives to retain free cash flow within the firm rather than to distribute it to shareholders. The benefits from using debt to address this problem are likely to be small for growth firms, since they have positive NPV projects in which to invest.[10]

The finding of a negative relation between leverage and the market-to-book ratio appears inconsistent with the Pecking Order Theory, which predicts a positive association between leverage and growth. Holding profitability (or internally generated cash) constant, a firm with greater investment opportunities will accumulate more debt over time.[11] But because the two theories are not mutually exclusive, the appropriate conclusion is that the Tradeoff Theory effect is larger than that of the Pecking Order Theory.

Alternative Proxies for Growth Options and Leverage. Because the market value of the firm appears on both the left- and right-hand sides of these regressions – in the denominator of the leverage ratio and in the numerator of the market-to-book ratio – some researchers have suggested that the strong negative relation between these variables is simply the "artificial" result of large variation in stock prices. To examine this concern, researchers have employed other proxies for corporate investment opportunities that do not rely on market values (for example, see Bradley, Jarrell and Kim, 1984 and Barclay and Smith, 2005). For instance, when R&D or advertising (each as a percentage of sales) is substituted for the firm's market-to-book ratio, the estimated coefficient has a negative sign and is highly significant, as predicted by the Tradeoff Theory.

Researchers also have estimated regressions using an alternative proxy for leverage – the interest coverage ratio (EBIT over interest expense) – a proxy that does not depend on stock prices. Although expected to produce less significant results (benefits of intangible growth opportunities are not reflected in current earnings), consistent with the Tradeoff Theory, companies with higher market-to-book ratios have significantly higher interest coverage ratios.

6.3.3   Leverage and firm size

The Tradeoff Theory suggests that larger firms will have proportionately more debt in their capital structures for at least two reasons. First, larger firms tend to be more diversified than smaller firms. Diversification reduces the volatility of a firm's cash flows and consequently its probability of becoming financially distressed. Second, there are economies of scale in bankruptcy filings; the direct costs are proportionally smaller for larger firms. The evidence that leverage is positively associated with firm size generally is interpreted as being consistent with the Tradeoff Theory.

The Pecking Order Theory's prediction with respect to firm size is debatable. Some argue that the theory predicts an inverse relation between leverage and firm size. Large firms are more likely than small firms to be known by investors; for example, larger firms have more analyst coverage (Bhushan, 1989). They consequently are less likely to suffer from asymmetric information problems when they announce new equity offerings (that is, they should experience a smaller drop in their stock prices when they announce new equity offerings). If these asymmetric information-based costs of equity are lower for larger firms, they should employ more equity financing and, thus, their leverage should be lower. Others argue that the Pecking Order Theory makes no prediction with respect to leverage and firm size. In either case, the evidence of a positive association between and firm size is consistent with the implications of the Tradeoff Theory and that the magnitude of the Tradeoff Theory effect is greater than that of the Pecking Order Theory.

6.3.4   Leverage and tangible assets

Tangible assets include such things as property, plant, equipment, and inventory. The Tradeoff Theory predicts a positive association between leverage and tangibility for at least three reasons. First, tangible assets serve as better collateral in lending agreements than intangible assets. Second, with more tangible assets, the Underinvestment Problem is less severe. Third, it can be to more difficult to substitute higher-risk assets for tangible assets; so, the Asset Substitution Problem is a less important concern.

Harris and Raviv (1991) argue that the Pecking Order Theory predicts a negative association between leverage and tangibility. They argue that in a firm whose value primarily reflects that of its tangible assets, there is less asymmetry of information between managers and outside investors. Correspondingly, these firms incur smaller asymmetric information costs when they make new equity offerings. And if equity is less costly, firms should use more of it. But others argue that this theory predicts no systematic association between leverage and tangibility. In any case, the observed positive association between tangibility and leverage implies that the Tradeoff Theory effect is greater than that of the Pecking Order Theory.

6.3.5   Leverage and profitability

The Tradeoff Theory suggests that leverage should be positively associated with firm profitability. Profitable firms are expected to have smaller financial distress costs – they can issue more debt while still maintaining a lower probability of distress. Profitability also potentially proxies for benefits of interest tax shields: If a firm has less taxable income, benefits from deducting the interest paid to debtholders are smaller.

Advocates of the Pecking Order Theory focus particular attention on the association between profitability and leverage ratios. They argue that highly profitable firms will have more internally generated cash to fund investment and thus will have lower leverage ratios than less profitable firms.

The observed negative association between leverage and profitability generally is interpreted as evidence against the Tradeoff Theory in favor of the Pecking Order Theory. Indeed, this finding typically is stressed when finance scholars discuss the apparent shortcomings of the Tradeoff Theory (for example, see Brealey, Myers and Allen, 2020). But again, these theories are not mutually exclusive. The estimated negative coefficient implies that the Pecking Order effect of profitability is greater than that implied by basic Tradeoff Models.

Some researchers, however, argue that profitable firms are likely to have more growth opportunities than less profitable firms (holding the market-to-book ratio and other variables constant). If so, the Tradeoff Theory also would suggest that they will have less debt in their capital structures. Perhaps more importantly, some dynamic tradeoff models of capital structure suggest a negative association between profitability and leverage.[12]

6.3.6   Cross-sectional versus time-series analysis

Lemmon, Roberts and Zender (2008) study all firms in the COMPUSTAT database over the period 1965 to 2003. They document that firm-level fixed effects alone explain 61% of the variation in market leverage ratios within their sample. Adding firm size, market-to book, profitability, and tangibility to the model, while statistically significant, only increases the explanatory power of the model to 68%. These findings suggest that much of the explanatory power in these models comes from cross-sectional, as opposed to time-series, variation.

Barclay, Smith and Watts (1995) estimate a purely cross-sectional model where they include only one observation for each of their 6,780 firms (the average value for each variable over their 30-year sample period). They continue to find a strong negative association between leverage and market-to-book and a strong positive association between leverage and firm size. The extended analysis of Lemmon, Roberts and Zender also suggests that time invariant differences in these variables (in addition to profitability and tangible assets) are significant in explaining firm-level capital structures.

Nonetheless, a substantial fraction of the firm-level fixed effect does not appear to be explained by our existing theories. It is possible that time-invariant differences in factors such as technologies, market power, and managerial behavior affect capital structure in ways that are not yet modeled or understood. These possibilities offer opportunities for future research.

6.3.7   Regulated firms

Although excluded from many studies, regulated firms offer potentially powerful tests of these capital structure theories. The Tradeoff Theory suggests that regulated firms (for example, banks, public utilities, and railroads) will have higher leverage ratios than otherwise similar unregulated firms. Regulation effectively reduces the opportunities for corporate underinvestment simply by transferring some of management's discretion over investment decisions to regulatory authorities. State utility commissions, for example, oversee utilities' investments in maintenance and capacity. Given such limits on managerial discretion – combined with the stability of cash flows assured by the regulatory process – regulated corporations are expected to have higher leverage targets than otherwise similar unregulated corporations.

Because the regulatory hearings typically are public events, the information disparity between managers and potential investors is lower. With the Information Asymmetry Problem better controlled, the costs of accessing equity markets are lower and, thus, the Pecking Order Theory would appear to imply that leverage for regulated firms should be lower.

The evidence in Barclay, Smith and Watts (1995), as well as various other studies, provides strong support for the hypothesis that regulated firms have significantly higher debt levels than unregulated firms. This finding suggests that the Tradeoff Theory effect is larger than that of the Pecking Order Theory effect.

Barclay, Smith and Watts also examine the change in leverage among telecommunications firms around the deregulation of their industry in 1982. They find that leverage averaged over 45% prior to deregulation but less than 25% afterwards. Ovtchinnikov (2010) also documents that firms experience significant changes in their operating environments following deregulation of their industries and that deregulated firms respond by reducing their leverage.

6.4   Other capital structure theories

We have concentrated on the two major capital structure theories: The Tradeoff Theory and the Pecking Order Theory. There is some evidence that other theories may help to explain aspects of firms' capital structure decisions.

6.4.1   Market Timing Theory

Taggert (1977) and others have provided evidence that firms tend to issue additional equity after a run-up in their stock prices. These findings are troublesome for the Pecking Order Theory since there is no reason to expect that managers will exhaust their available debt capacity when stock prices are "high." This evidence is also problematic for the Tradeoff Theory. As Myers (1984) notes: "If firm value rises, the debt-to-value ratio falls, and firms ought to issue debt, not equity, to rebalance their capital structures."

Baker and Wurgler (2002) argue that this evidence of equity issues following stock price increases implies managers try to time stock issues to occur when security prices are "high"; in fact, in their paper they assume that the sole motive for corporate equity offerings is to time the market to sell overvalued shares to less-informed investors. Their *Market Timing Theory* potentially helps to explain why aggregate stock issues increase in bull markets and fall in bear markets.

But, as discussed in Chapter 5, the Market Timing Theory faces a daunting challenge, precisely because of the "lemons problem" identified by Nobel laureate George Akerlof (1970). For example, suppose for all the firms with overvalued shares, the publicly known average overvaluation was 2%, and all these firms announced Seasoned Equity Offerings (SEOs). Upon announcements of the offerings, rational investors would lower their estimates of the firms' values by 2%. But this price adjustment would eliminate the presumed motive for the SEO for all the firms with overvaluations less than 2%. If only firms with an overvaluation greater than 2% announced SEOs, then the appropriate price revision by rational investors would be greater. Were this the only motive for SEOs, as assumed by Baker and Wurgler, this market would collapse, and these transactions simply would not be observed. Thus, this cannot be the primary driver of SEOs.[13]

In the next chapter, we present a potential explanation for the finding that SEOs tend to occur after stock price run-ups that is consistent with a dynamic version of the Tradeoff Theory – *Strategic Financial Management*.

6.4.2   Signaling models

As discussed in Chapter 5, Ross (1977) presents a formal signaling model in which a higher level of debt credibly conveys positive inside information about the firm to outside investors. Ross focuses on this signaling problem at a fairly high level of abstraction and offers no suggestion as to how this effect might be measured empirically. Barclay, Smith and Watts (1995) provide some evidence on capital structure signaling. Although their coefficient has the appropriate sign, its significance level is relatively low. Potentially more concerning, however, their results imply that if one were to move from the 10th percentile to the 90th percentile in their proxy for signaling, the implied change in target leverage would be one half of one percent. This result raises two issues: First, because it is difficult to identify when managers have such proprietary (and thus largely unobservable) information, it is challenging to test this proposition. If researchers employ a noisy proxy for signaling, their estimate will understate the real effect. Second, given this estimated magnitude, managers might reasonably conclude that the benefits of signaling might be so small that it is not worth the effort. Thus, we believe that signaling results to date should be considered as simply suggestive.

6.4.3   Behavioral motives

Bertrand and Schoar (2003) provide evidence that supports various behavioral explanations of corporate financial decisions. They find that individual "styles" persist as CEOs and CFOs move between firms. Older CEOs tend to be more conservative in issuing debt than younger CEOS, while those with MBAs tend to be less conservative than those without the degree. This behavioral theory, however, has little to say about factors that might explain firms' choices of high versus low leverage.

6.5   Market reactions to announcements of security offerings

Outside investors recognize that managers invariably have superior information about their firm's prospects and reasonably fear that managers might time new security issues to sell overvalued securities to less-informed investors. Recognizing this potential problem, investors are likely to lower the price they are willing to pay for the firms' new, as well as its existing, securities. This downward price adjustment is likely to be greatest for securities whose prices are most sensitive to information about the firm's prospects – common stock and convertible securities.

As we discussed earlier, informational asymmetries and the resulting *adverse selection problem* are fundamental underpinnings of the Pecking Order Theory.[14] According to this theory, managers prefer to fund investment with internally generated funds to avoid security price reductions.

Table 6.4   The stock market response to announcements of
                 security offers

	Type of issuer	
Type of security offer	Industrial	Utility
Common stock	-3.14%* (155)	-0.75%* (403)
Straight bonds	-0.26% (248)	-0.13% (140)
Convertible bonds	-2.07%*	n.a. (73)

This table shows the average two-day abnormal common stock returns and average sample size (in parentheses) from event studies of announcements of security offerings. Returns are weighted averages based on sample size.
Note: * indicates statistically significantly different from zero.
Source: This table presents a subset of the results reported in Table 1 of Smith (1986a). The average returns are based on multiple research studies. See Smith for the underlying references.

When they are "forced" to issue new securities, they prefer to issue debt over equity, in large part because an announcement of an equity sale is likely to generate the more negative market reaction.

Table 6.4 presents a summary of the findings of academic research on the market's response to announcements of public issues grouped by industrial firms and utilities for the various types of securities typically sold.[15] Consistent with asymmetric information arguments, the average abnormal returns (that is, price movements adjusted for general market price changes) are consistently either negative or not significantly different from zero – in no case is there evidence of a significant positive reaction. Furthermore, the market's response to announcements of common stock issues by firms is more strongly negative than its response to straight debt offerings. It is also more negative to announcements of convertible than non-convertible securities, and more negative to announcements of offerings by industrials than utilities. Again, as regulated firms, utilities potentially face less severe informational disparities than might the typical industrial firm.

It is important for managers to understand the market reactions to the announcements of new security issues; they represent a potentially important cost. In the next chapter, we discuss circumstances under which managers might mitigate these negative effects.

6.6   Conclusions

At the most general level, there are at least two primary theories of how firms manage their capital structures: The Tradeoff Theory and the Pecking Order Theory. The Tradeoff Theory argues that firms have target capital structures that depend on the specific incremental costs and benefits they face from employing debt. The Pecking Order Theory argues that managers have a strict preference for internal over external financing and debt over equity financing when the firm has to raise funds externally. Under versions of this theory, firms do not have target capital structures – observed capital structures are simply the result of past investment requirements and financing history.

Within this chapter we reviewed the collective evidence from large-sample panel studies that are directed at testing alternative capital structure theories. The results from these studies do not support the most basic tradeoff models which hold investment policy fixed. They report little evidence of an important role for direct bankruptcy costs, consistent with expected direct costs of bankruptcy being quite small for most public corporations. And there is comparably little evidence that the firm's current marginal tax rate is a major determinant of a firm's capital structure.

The collective evidence provides reasonably strong support for versions of tradeoff models that focus on the indirect costs of financial distress, including the Underinvestment Problem and the Free Cash-Flow (Overinvestment) Problem. Leverage appears to be significantly and negatively related to the firm's market-to-book ratio, a widely employed proxy for the firm's growth opportunities. According to the Tradeoff Theory, growth firms will use less debt in their capital structures because of greater concerns about the indirect costs of financial distress, particularly the Underinvestment Problem. At the same time, they gain fewer benefits from using debt to address the Overinvestment Problem, which by definition occurs primarily in low-growth "value" firms. The observed positive association between leverage and the tangibility of assets, firm size, and regulatory status, provide additional support for the Tradeoff Theory.

Advocates for the Pecking Order Theory frequently focus on the observed negative relation between leverage and firm profitability. The Pecking Order Theory predicts this relation. In contrast, consideration of the tax benefits of debt and the costs of financial distress produces the opposite prediction under the standard Tradeoff Theory. (There are, however, recent more complex dynamic models of the Tradeoff Theory that might help to explain this finding.)

The empirical research, while generally supporting a version of the Tradeoff Theory, does not imply that the Pecking Order Theory is incorrect or unimportant, nor that asymmetric information between managers and outside investors can be ignored. Because the Tradeoff and Pecking Order Theories are not mutually exclusive, both effects can be important and the observed regression coefficients simply reflect the algebraic sum of the various effects. Thus, a result of no association might be a result of offsetting effects.

Managers rightfully are concerned about the strong negative stock market reactions that often greet the announcements of new equity offerings (as summarized in this chapter). These concerns might be an additional reason beyond the Overinvestment Problem for why large, mature firms with access to public bond markets rarely issue equity. Moreover, evidence suggests that the typical manager's financing preferences have the ordering implied by the theory, the major implication of the Pecking Order Theory. But this ordering also aligns with the costs of accessing these markets. Nonetheless, the collective evidence suggest that many firms have target leverage ratios that vary across firms and time in a reasonably predictable fashion.

Currently there is no comprehensive theory to explain how firms choose their capital structures. However, existing Tradeoff Theories, coupled with the empirical evidence, provide useful managerial insights. Financial managers appear to and probably should consider their firms' expected costs from financial distress and incentive-related agency issues in establishing their firm's target leverage. The firm's investment opportunity set, the tangibility of the firm's assets, firm size, and regulatory status appear to be particularly important considerations. Taxes while not being a primary determinant of capital structure for the typical firm still may have some importance.

While our understanding of capital structure decisions has greatly increased since the middle of the 20th century when serious research on the topic began, there is still much that is unexplained by existing theories and models. This creates valuable opportunities for future research.

Notes

1. Static models focus on a single time period. More recently, researchers have begun to develop dynamic tradeoff models (for example, Titman and Tsyplakov, 2007) where financing decisions in the current period depend on the firm's expectations about future profits, payouts, investment, financing, etc. Our focus in this chapter is on static models, which to date have played a more prominent role in the finance literature. In the next chapter, we present a dynamic version of the Tradeoff Theory – *Strategic Financial Management*. "Tradeoff Theory," refers to a group of related theoretical models or explanations that vary in the emphasized costs and benefits of debt. For example, the early tradeoff models held investment policy fixed and focused on the tax benefits of debt and the direct bankruptcy costs, while later models have placed more emphasis on the indirect costs of financial distress and various incentive-related issues, such as the Underinvestment and Overinvestment Problems.
2. Random events, such as a change in the firm's market value, can move a firm away from its target capital structure (assuming it has one). The Tradeoff Theory generally assumes that there are costs in adjusting back toward that target, and so this adjustment does not occur immediately but occurs over time, for example, as the firm seeks additional financing from external capital markets.
3. The argument that managers have these strict preferences has been in the finance literature for many years (for example, Donaldson, 1961). However, it has gained increased acceptance among finance scholars following more recent theoretical work on the effects of informational asymmetries between inside managers and outside investors and associated adverse selection problems on the pricing of securities (see Myers and Majluf, 1984). Consistent with the underlying assumptions of this theory, the typical firm experiences a significant stock price decline when it announces a new equity offering (Asquith and Mullins., 1986; Masulis and Korwar, 1986), while ordinary bond issues on average are greeted with insignificant market reactions (Eckbo, 1986). Adverse selection and stock market reactions to new security issues are discussed in greater detail later in this chapter.

4. Much of the evidence on capital structure is based on the analysis of panel datasets. Other evidence comes from studies of financing decisions at the aggregate level, leverage changes, the market reactions to leverage changes, so-called "natural experiments," and surveys. We focus primarily in this chapter on the evidence from panel studies with some discussion of the market reactions to announcements of new security issues. For a more general summary of empirical research on capital structure, see Frank and Goyal (2008).

5. For example, Barclay and Smith (2005), Barclay, Smith and Watts (1995), Bradley, Jarrell and Kim (1984), Crutchley and Hansen (1989), Frank and Goyal (2009), Graham, Leary and Roberts (2015), Lemmon, Roberts and Zender (2008), Long and Malitz (1985), Oztekin (2015), Rajan and Zingales (1995), Smith and Watts (1992), and Titman and Wessels (1988).

6. In addition to these four variables, the median leverage ratio for the industry and, to a lesser degree, expected inflation have consistent explanatory power. Exactly for what the median industry leverage ratio is proxying remains unclear. It could proxy for a variety of omitted variables, which might affect capital structure (for example, relating to product market interactions). Including this variable in the model affects the estimated coefficients of the other key variables but does not have a large effect on their signs or significance levels (see Lemmon, Roberts and Zender, 2008, table 2).

7. Barclay, Heitzman and Smith (2013) provide evidence from the real estate industry where differences in tax rates across organizational forms present a potential opportunity for more powerful tests concerning the importance of entity-level taxes in capital structure decisions. Their evidence suggests that, although taxes do seem to matter, their role is clearly secondary to factors such as the nature of the firm's assets.

8. The authors report generally similar results using book leverage as the dependent variable. However, the R^2s are lower and the significance levels somewhat less consistent. For their full sample, book leverage becomes negatively and significantly associated with the market-to-book ratio only after 1980. Size, profitability, and tangible assets are generally significant and of the same sign as in the market leverage regressions in most decades.

9. The following discussion draws on Frank and Goyal (2008). Note that the predictions for each of the underlying variables are either suggested by the existing literature or are derived logically from what might be expected on an *a priori* basis under each theory. Since neither of the theories is completely specified and a proxy intended to capture an underlying variable might proxy for something else, it is likely that a proponent of either theory can rationalize an apparent contrary result on an *ex-post* basis. Some of these rationalizations are discussed below.

10. Barclay, Morellec, and Smith (2006) incorporate both the Underinvestment Problem and the Overinvestment Problem into one theoretical model. Their model predicts that the total dollar amount of debt in a firm's capital structure will decline with an additional growth option, even though firm value increases with the new investment opportunity. "The logic that produces this conclusion is straightforward. Other things equal, if the value of the firm increases with additional growth options (with no change to the assets

in place), the underinvestment costs of debt increase and the free cash-flow benefits of debt decline. These higher costs and lower benefits of debt generated by the addition of growth options cause a reduction in the optimal amount of total debt even though firm value is rising." Their empirical evidence is consistent with this prediction.

11. Some advocates of the Pecking Order Theory assert that the market-to-book ratio is simply an additional proxy for firm profitability (providing information about profits beyond what is in reported accounting profits, which are included in the typical regression). For the reasons discussed below, the Pecking Order Theory predicts a negative association between leverage and profits (Brealey, Myers and Allen, 2020). Thus, they argue that the observed association is consistent with this theory. Researchers, however, have found that leverage is negatively and significantly related to other measures of growth opportunities, such as expenditures on advertising and R&D, which presumably are not proxies for profits (see our subsequent discussion).

12. See Frank and Goyal, 2008, p. 146, for example.

13. The lemons argument does not imply that senior corporate managers engage in no forms of market timing. Investment projects frequently involve proprietary information – information that is potentially more valuable to competitors than to investors. For this reason, firms do not always immediately disclose all relevant information about an investment (see Lys, Kothari, Smith, and Watts, 1988). Because of this information disparity between managers and investors, in an efficient capital market, prices should reflect an unbiased assessment of value based on the available information.

14. Adverse selection refers to the tendency of an individual with private information about something that affects a potential trading partner's costs and benefits to extend an offer that would be detrimental to the trading partner. See Akerlof (1970).

15. A public company seeking external capital must first decide what type of claim to sell. In making that decision, it is important to understand the market's typical reaction to the announcements of these transactions. In a reasonably efficient market, the stock market's reaction to the securities offering will be centered, not at its execution, but around the announcement of the transaction – the event where the release of new information is greatest.

7   Strategic financial management

Although corporate finance has been a central part of the taught curriculum in business schools for more than a century, the academic finance community still finds it difficult to provide definitive answers to three fundamental questions concerning capital structure: (1) Given a total level of capital necessary to support a firm's activities, is there a way of dividing up that capital into debt and equity that maximizes firm value? (2) Do firms have target leverage ratios, and if so, what are the critical factors in determining the optimal target? (3) How should a firm manage its financing decisions given a leverage target?

In the first six chapters of this book, our primary focus has been on the first two questions. We discussed two major theories that have been developed to help answer these two questions: the Tradeoff Theory and the Pecking Order Theory. In addition, we presented the Market Timing that some scholars advocate. In this chapter, we turn to the third question of managing a firm's financing policy. Our examination of the evidence on how firms manage their financing decisions provides additional evidence on these three basic theories, identifies material inconsistencies in each of them, and offers an alternative theory: Strategic Financial Management. Developed by Barclay, Fu and Smith (2021), this theory appears to retain the productive aspects of the other three theories but avoids their major problems.

7.1   Raising capital[1]

Firms raise external capital by selling an array of different securities. Common stock, straight and convertible debt, preferred and convertible preferred stock are the main forms of claims that are underwritten by investment bankers in capital markets. In this section, we discuss the process by which financial securities are created and marketed. There is a sequence of steps that firms typically go through in the process of having a public securities offering. Below we lay out the typical sequence of events for a public equity offering. We focus on publicly traded firms with existing shares traded in the capital market. Consistent with the evidence presented in the previous chapter, we assume that the typical firm has a target leverage ratio.

7.1.1   Public equity offering: the initial steps

In considering the firm's sources and uses of funds, if the CFO finds there is a shortfall, external sources of funds will be considered. If there are reasons to question the type of security that the firm should sell, the investment banker – typically one with whom the firm has an established relationship – is called. Non-Disclosure Agreements (NDAs or Confidentiality Agreements) are signed, and the CFO lays out both the firm's current and anticipated future circumstances for the investment banker.

If a public equity issue is selected, this decision requires ratification by the board of directors. An underwriting agreement with the investment banker is signed, and (if it hasn't already occurred) a securities law firm is retained. The firm's internal finance, accounting, and legal teams, as well as its external public accounting firm, will begin to assist the security lawyers and investment bankers in preparing a filing to be submitted to the Securities and Exchange Commission (SEC). The investment bankers will work to complete their due diligence responsibilities and will begin to assemble a group of investment banking and retail brokerage firms to populate the syndicate – a special-purpose partnership to market the securities to the public. Again, NDAs are signed by all.

7.1.2   SEC filing

Thus far, everything has been done without public disclosure, but a security filing with the SEC is a public document. Thus, on the filing date, the firm typically issues a press release stating that it intends to have a *seasoned equity offering* (SEO).[2]

The SEC reviews the filing and either declares the filing "effective" or "deficient." (For firms working with experienced investment bankers and securities lawyers, deficiency notices are extremely rare.) While the issue is in registration, permitted communication with the public is restricted. The company can announce the SEO by taking out a "tombstone ad" (what can be included is quite limited, so it has a lot of white space – like information on a tombstone). The firm and syndicate members can distribute a preliminary prospectus (generally called a "red herring" prospectus; it must include a statement that the SEC has not approved the filing printed in red ink on its front page).

During this period, members of the syndicate are permitted to contact potential investors, and if an investor appears receptive the investment banker records an "indication of interest" (also called a "circle"). Under U.S. securities law, no binding agreement between the syndicate member and the investor to purchase shares at the offering is permitted.

7.1.3   The effective date

When the firm is notified that the registration statement is effective, several things happen in rapid succession: the offer date is set – generally for some time after the opening on the next day. But if the firm's story is complicated, the offer date might be set a few days later to allow time to put on a *road show*.[3] But for most offerings, this option goes unexercised.

A *due diligence* meeting is set, frequently for that evening. Each party who plays a material role in the SEO (the firm's senior executives, the securities law firm, the public accounting firm, members of the underwriting syndicate, etc.) will have an authorized representative present, and each must attest to the nature of the role that their firm played. At some level, this is a meeting to limit the legal liability of the various participants.

The offer price is set. Although this contract is called a firm-commitment underwriting agreement, there is little in the way of a price guarantee. The offer price is rarely set earlier than the close on the day before the offering, and sometimes only after the open the morning of the offer. Under the *Rules of Fair Practice* of the National Association of Security Dealers, once the offer price is set, syndicate members are precluded from selling the shares at a higher price. They can sell the shares at a lower price only if the syndicate "breaks" – a rare occurrence.

7.1.4   The offer date

When the appointed hour arrives, potential investors who have given a syndicate member an indication of interest are called. Offers frequently are fully subscribed within an hour or so.

7.1.5   The aftermath

Following full subscription, the syndicate begins to wrap things up. Investors who purchased shares pay. The CFO typically receives access to the proceeds several days after the offering, allowing brokers time for investors to pay for their shares. At that point, the syndicate is dissolved.

7.2   Costs associated with security offerings

Raising external equity capital is expensive. For this reason, a firm, after selecting a leverage target, expects to deviate from that target over time. If the firm's current leverage is not at its target level, the CFO will consider not just the benefits of moving toward its target but also any associated adjustment costs. As a general principle, the CFO is expected to adjust the firm's capital structure whenever the costs of adjustment are less than the costs of deviating from its target. (For instance, suppose that current leverage is above its target and the opportunity cost of that deviation is, say, 1% of firm value. But if the cost of a leverage-adjusting transaction were 2%, the firm would not adjust – the costs outweigh the potential benefits.)

Leverage-adjustment costs include both out-of-pocket transactions costs and information-related costs. As discussed in the previous chapter, the price of a firm's shares typically falls when an SEO is announced – presumably due to asymmetric information between managers and shareholders (as predicted by the Pecking Order Theory). The magnitudes of both out-of-pocket transactions and information-related costs are important considerations when making financing decisions.

Evidence suggests that there is a substantial fixed component of these costs, and among different sources of external capital, these fixed costs vary substantially. Equity issues have both the largest out-of-pocket transactions costs and the largest information costs; long-term public debt issues are next most costly; and short-term private debt is the least costly (especially when drawing against an established bank credit line). Because CFOs weigh these adjustment costs against the expected benefits of moving closer to their leverage target, larger adjustment costs will lead to larger deviations from the target before the firm adjusts. This, in turn, implies that SEOs should be relatively rare events; long-term bond issues are somewhat more frequent, and draws against bank credit lines occur with great regularity. But for our purposes, the most important implication is because of the structure of these adjustment costs, a firm's leverage will rarely be at its target level.

To illustrate this point, let's consider a very simple special case: Suppose (1) the firm has a target leverage of 25% debt (as a fraction of the market value of the firm's assets), (2) the firm's "debt capacity" – that leverage where the opportunity cost of deviating from target leverage outweighs the costs of adjusting its leverage – is 30%, (3) new positive NPV projects are equal in size and developed at a constant rate, and there is no uncertainty about the value of these projects nor their expected future cash flows, (4) internally generated cash is insufficient to fund them, and (5) a bank credit line and new equity sales are the firm's only two sources of external funds. Because accessing the bank line involves lower costs than having an equity offering, the firm will fund these new projects with draws against its line of credit until its debt capacity is reached. At this point, the firm will have an equity offering to reduce its leverage. But because the costs of an equity offering have a substantial fixed component as well as significant scale economies, the offering will not be sized to take the firm to its leverage target. The offering size is likely to be larger – it will "over-shoot" its target leverage. In this special case, a graph of the firm's leverage against time will trace a saw-tooth pattern: Leverage will rise until it reaches the firm's debt capacity, at which time it will have an equity offering, dropping leverage below its target level; then it again will start to rise.

But there is an important omission in this story; it assumes the only reason that a firm would have an equity offering is because it has reached its debt capacity –the transaction is undertaken to adjust its leverage. In the next section, we relax this assumption and consider why firms with excess debt capacity undertake SEOs.

7.3   Strategic Financial Management – an overview[4]

Perhaps the most distinctive and valuable feature of the Barclay, Fu and Smith (BFS) analysis is its focus on the interaction between a firm's investment and financing decisions. The evidence from SEOs suggests that equity financing, far from serving simply as a leverage-adjustment tool, is triggered primarily by the development of a large growth opportunity. The size of its associated capital requirements and expected cash inflows from exercising this growth option are critical determinants of the choice between debt and equity.

7.3.1   The basic idea

Consider a firm contemplating a large investment project that will take several years to complete. Were the firm to finance the entire project with debt, prior to project completion, it would exceed its target leverage by an unacceptable amount – it would exceed the company's debt capacity. The firm might decide first to borrow until its debt capacity is exhausted, as the Pecking Order Theory suggests. However, adherence to the pecking order has the potential to create a large Underinvestment Problem. As Myers (1977) argues, in highly levered firms, the priority of debt can create circumstances where lenders capture enough of the benefits of a positive NPV project, that what is left for stockholders fails to provide a normal return for the capital they commit and the risk they assume (see Chapter 5).

BFS suggest that in these circumstances, firms typically sell equity in the early stages of such projects. And they do so even when they appear to be operating well below their leverage targets. In such cases, the equity offerings have the effect of moving the firms further from, not closer to, their long-run target leverage. But subsequent financings are debt issues that finance the completion of the project and have the longer-run effect of moving these companies back toward their leverage targets.

A Brief Overview of the Empirical Findings. In a study of 8,608 SEOs by U.S. companies from January 1970 to December 2015 BFS reached the following conclusions:

- For the average SEO firm, the level of corporate investment increases substantially in the quarter of the SEO and remains high during at least the next five years. For the majority of issuers, the increase in corporate investment during the three years following the SEO exceeds the net proceeds from the offering.

- During the three-year period leading up to the SEO, the average issuer's leverage tends to be well below its leverage target, and, mainly because of increases in the firm's stock price, its economic leverage is falling. In the quarter of the SEO, leverage falls further from the infusion of new equity.
- During the five years following the SEO, driven primarily by the issuance of substantial amounts of debt, the typical issuer's leverage increases above its pre-SEO level.

7.3.2   Why have an SEO?

Two Basic Motives for SEOs. These basic findings suggest that most equity issuers are firms whose values in large part reflect what Myers has called growth options – BFS classify roughly 62% of their industrial SEO firms as "growth firms."[5] Approximately 10% are "value companies" whose assets in place generate a high level of cash flows. Unlike the growth firms, these value firms typically have higher leverage as well as smaller but more regular growth opportunities – although the investment project that prompts their SEOs appears similar in size to those of the growth SEO firms. The leverage of these value companies is more likely to be above their target levels, thus rebalancing their capital structures appears to be a more prominent motive for their SEOs – more like what a standard tradeoff model would suggest.

The Importance for Finance Theory. These findings are fundamentally inconsistent with most current theories of financial management:

- In contrast to the predictions of the Tradeoff Theory, SEOs often move firms away from rather than closer to their leverage targets. In the periods leading up to their SEOs, information about their new investment opportunities typically increases their stock prices and thereby reduces their leverage.
- Contrary to the Pecking Order Theory, companies do not exhaust other financing alternatives before issuing equity – equity simply does not appear to be "the financing instrument of last resort." Indeed, the majority of SEO firms are growth firms that are financially robust with low leverage and often substantial unused debt capacity.

- Most SEOs are motivated by the external capital requirements of large investment projects rather than by market-timing considerations.
- SEO issuers issue significant amounts of debt following their SEO, this is explicitly ruled out by both the Market Timing Theory and more extreme versions of the Pecking Order Theory; each assumes that a firm has no leverage target and thus no reason to "rebalance" its capital structure after an SEO.

Unlike the BFS concept of Strategic Financial Management, the Tradeoff, Pecking Order and Market Timing theories each effectively assumes that managers behave "myopically" when implementing corporate financial policy. Tradeoff theories, for example, typically assume that a firm's investment opportunities and cash flows are stationary, which would imply that the company's leverage target is constant. More sophisticated dynamic models of the Tradeoff Theory incorporate adjustment costs and allow for temporary deviations from the firm's leverage target. But there is little consideration within these models of the possibility that a company might issue equity when its leverage ratio is below its target level.

Sequencing Financing Transactions. BFS's findings suggest that managers consider their companies' investment plans and associated capital requirements over a long horizon and choose a sequence of financing transactions to maximize firm value by ensuring an adequate supply of equity capital across an array of potential investment outcomes. In managing corporate financing policy, CFOs consider both their projected balance sheets and cash-flow statements over the foreseeable future. And in their analysis, CFOs may conclude that issuing equity, even when the current level of leverage is well below target, helps preserve value by reinforcing their firms' commitment to fund a major project that could require large investments over multiple periods. As the project moves toward completion, their growth options are exercised, gradually transforming them into assets in place. Over this period, the CFO plans to issue debt. Such debt offerings, moreover, can be expected to command more favorable terms that reflect both the reduction in default risk from the prior equity infusion, its associated realization of payoffs from the project, as well as more effective control of the Underinvestment Problem.

SEOs and Underinvestment. Following the Pecking Order Theory can create a major Underinvestment Problem. In a highly levered firm, the priority of debt claims creates the potential for lenders to capture enough of the benefits of a positive NPV project that the cash flows left for the equityholders fail to provide a return sufficient to compensate them for the capital they have contributed and the level of risk that they bear. By initially issuing debt, the firm raises the likelihood of walking away from a positive NPV project (or scaling back by substituting a less expensive but less valuable project) if either the anticipated value of the project and the value of the entire firm falls prior to project completion.

The company reinforces its commitment to carry out its entire sequence of future planned investment expenditures by first having an SEO. This more effective control of the underinvestment problem increases future expected cash flows to the stockholders and thus equity values. The firm's debt becomes less risky since it is supported by greater equity claims and thus would be priced on more attractive terms.[6]

In summary, for a CFO tasked with financing a large multi-year investment program that will require raising both debt and equity capital, the value-maximizing financing sequence is likely to be equity, then debt. Even if current leverage were below target, the company still should have the equity offering first, understanding that following the SEO financing employed to complete the project will be debt issues to move the firm nearer its target capital structure.

Investment Opportunities, SEOs, and Financial Management. Large corporate investment projects typically are preceded by positive news about their development, and hence rising stock prices (McConnell and Muscarella, 1985). The Market Timing Theory argues that the rising stock price is evidence of overpriced shares and, in this sense, that rising stock prices cause the SEO. We suggest that it is the development and disclosure of the investment opportunities that both cause the stock price to rise and motivate the firm to have the SEO. In this view, the observed relation between stock price changes and SEOs is one of correlation, not causation – both are caused by the same triggering event.

Baker and Wurgler (2002), in their support of the Market Timing Theory, point to the excess returns that managers obtain when they buy or sell their firm's shares; they suggest that an SEO provides similar opportunities to exploit their private information by selling overvalued shares to less-informed investors. However, as we have discussed, this analogy is inappropriate for one major reason. Insider trades are announced only after the fact – after the trade has occurred. But SEOs are widely publicized before the shares are offered for sale to investors. Within a reasonably efficient market, skeptical investors will be concerned about the possibility of managers attempting to exploit their informational advantage in an SEO. Presumably they will ask themselves: *Is management raising equity primarily because it has a valuable use for the funds or because it believes the firm's shares are overvalued, as the Market Timing Theory suggests?* These investors have strong incentives to "price-protect" themselves when trading with a party who clearly has better information than they have.

This argument implies that if market timing motives were the sole reason for SEOs, that the market would implode – we simply would see no SEOs. For this reason, management is careful to announce, either in the offering prospectus or through other channels, that they have productive uses of the funds. By paring a major investment project with the proceeds of an SEO, managers make a more credible case to potential investors that the purpose of the SEO is to fund the project, not to stuff the portfolios of less-informed investors with overpriced shares.

7.4   Evidence from SEOs

BFS examine 7,039 SEOs announced by U.S. industrial firms over the period 1970 to 2015. The industries that are most frequently represented are: pharmaceutical (1,048 SEOs), oil (615), electronic equipment (519), retail (420), software (382), business services (381), and medical equipment (305). In addition, their sample includes 1,569 utility company SEOs over the same period.

7.4.1   Financial condition of SEO firms

Table 7.1 reports summary statistics for SEO proceeds, as a proportion of the firm's market value in year -1, and the market-to-book asset ratio for year -1 for the industrial and utility firms in the BFS sample. For industrial firms, SEOs average almost 19% of the issuing firm's total market value (book debt plus market equity at the end of the year prior to the SEO), implying the offering would have a substantial impact on the issuer's capital structure. Utility issues are smaller, averaging just

5%. The average market-to-book assets for industrial SEO firms is 2.75, which implies that the value of the typical industrial SEO firm reflects a substantial growth-option component in its investment opportunity set. At 1.07, this component is much smaller for utilities. The SEO firms are generally larger for both industrials and utilities than the typical firms in their industries (using the Fama-French 49-industry classification).

Table 7.1   Summary statistics of SEO proceeds and firm characteristics

Variables	Industrial SEOs			Utility SEOs		
	Mean	Median	Std. Dev.	Mean	Median	Std. Dev.
SEO Proceeds/ Market Value in Year -1	0.187	0.134	0.239	0.05	0.036	0.062
Market-to-Book Asset Ratio in Year -1	2.752	1.824	2.456	1.067	0.954	0.609

SEO proceeds are measured by multiplying the number of new shares by the offer price. The market value of assets in the fiscal year prior to the offering, measured by the book value of asset minus the book value of equity plus the market value of equity. Book value of equity is COMPUSTAT's total assets, minus total liabilities, plus balance sheet deferred taxes and investment tax credit, minus liquidation, redemption, or carrying value of preferred stock if available in the order. Market value of equity is obtained from CRSP's monthly stock return file, computed as the product of share price and shares outstanding. The sample has 7,039 industrial SEOs and 1,569 utility SEOs during 1970–2015.
Source: This table presents a subset of the results reported in Table 1 of Barclay, Fu and Smith (2021).

Table 7.2 presents the financial conditions of the industrial firms in the BFS sample in the three-year period leading up to their SEOs. For the median firm, market leverage declines over the pre-offering period (due largely to a run-up in the firm's stock price). The interest coverage and current ratios are relatively strong in all years, and the market-to-book ratio increases over the period and is substantially greater than one. Furthermore, the Altman Z score, which frequently is used as a predictor of bankruptcy, is above 3.0 in all years, which suggests a very low probability of bankruptcy. Statistical tests reveal that the typical SEO firm has lower leverage, a higher current ratio, a higher market-to-book ratio, and a higher Z-score than its industry peers (using the Fama-French industry classification). Overall, the evidence strongly suggests that the typical firm is not in financial distress leading up to the SEO.

The Pecking Order Theory suggests that SEO firms should be financially constrained with high leverage. The data in Table 7.2 appear to be completely inconsistent with that prediction – they simply do not describe a firm that is issuing equity as a last resort. Moreover, the leverage of the typical SEO firm is falling prior to the offering. These facts are at odds with standard versions of the Tradeoff Theory, which suggest that equity issues should move leverage toward its target. Therefore, both the time series and the cross-sectional evidence appears inconsistent with central implications of both theories. However, this evidence is quite consistent with Strategic Financial Management, which suggests that the primary function of the SEO is to finance large new investments.

Table 7.2   The financial condition of industrial SEO firms prior to the offering

Year relative to SEO	Market leverage	Interest coverage ratio	Current ratio	Market-to-book assets	Altman Z-score
-3	0.153	2.614	2.225	1.457	3.211
-2	0.148	2.493	2.196	1.543	3.244
-1	0.127	2.683	2.144	1.824	3.503

The table reports median financial ratios of industrial SEO firms in three years preceding the SEO and Wilcoxon test results of the median differences in financial ratios between year -1 and year -3 and between the SEO firm and its associated industry median at year -1. Industry is classified into 49 groups as proposed by Fama and French.

7.4.2   Investment dynamics around SEOs

The top panel of Figure 7.1 shows that investment as a percentage of total firm value in year -1 increases substantially following industrial firm SEOs. The increase in investment displayed in this figure is significantly larger for the average industrial SEO company than for the typical COMPUSTAT firm matched based on a comparable market-to-book ratio in the prior year. Fu and Smith's (2021) comparison of industrial SEO companies with these matched control firms reveals that the average annual "excess" investment during the three years following the SEO is 7.5% of total book assets. And the net excess increase in annual investment following the SEO was more than 50% for the median issuer. As a result of this substantial increase in investment, the median SEO company experiences an excess increase in book assets from the year prior to two years following the SEO of over 50% and an excess increase of 31.5% in the market value of assets. Not only are these ratios higher than the COMPUSTAT medians, but they are also positively skewed.

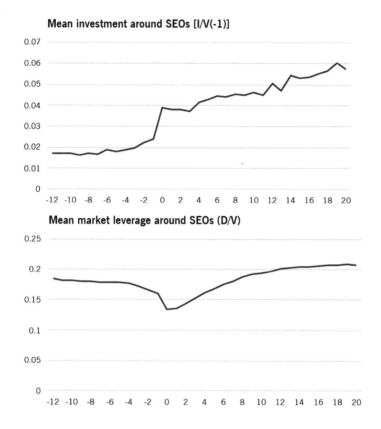

Figure 7.1   Changes in investment and leverage over time of SEO industrial firms

Source: Figure 1 in Fu and Smith, 2021 (permission to reprint).
The two panels in this graph respectively show the mean ratios of investment to firm value and market leverage from 12 quarters before the SEO to 20 quarters after the SEO. The quarter that SEOs take place is defined as quarter 0. Debt (D) is the sum of the long-term debt and the short-term debt (debt in current liabilities). Investment (I) is the sum of capital expenditure and if any, acquisition expenses and other increases in investment. The investment is deflated by the market value of the SEO firm in the quarter before the SEO (V(-1)).

This implies that the highest quartile of SEO firms invested even more aggressively after the offering.

7.4.3 Leverage dynamics around SEOs

Leverage Changes prior to SEOs. As shown in the bottom panel of Figure 7.1, from three years before an industrial firm SEO until about nine months prior to the offering, average market leverage is quite stable at approximately 18%, the median is 14%. Thereafter, it begins to fall. This decline is driven by the substantial increase in the firms' stock prices during the six months preceding the offering. The buy-and-hold abnormal return for the stocks in this sample is 37% over this six-month window (see section 7.4.6). This increase in stock prices is consistent with the results reported by McConnell and Muscarella (1985), who report a significant increase in stock prices for firms that report substantial increases in capital investment programs. By contrast, throughout the entire three-year period prior to the offering, book leverage – which should not be affected by stock price changes – remains quite stable.

Leverage Changes in the SEO Quarter. The infusion of equity from the SEO causes average market leverage to fall from 16% in the quarter before the offering to 13.5% by the end of the quarter of the offering. (Average book leverage drops from 25.5% to 19.5% over this same period.) Given that the offering increases the average number of shares outstanding by approximately 21%, this reduction should not be surprising.

Leverage Changes Following SEOs. Following the offering, this decline is reversed. Over the succeeding three years, average market leverage rises above its pre-SEO level to 20% and continues to rise. (Book leverage similarly rises to 25%.) Of course, there are two ways that leverage might increase – from an increase in debt or a reduction in equity. And equity can decline either from share repurchases or from stock price declines. But SEO firms rarely repurchase shares in the years immediately following the SEO. In fact, during the 12 quarters following the offering, average shares outstanding rise slightly. Now buy-and-hold returns over this window are negative 18%, and this certainly accounts for part of the increase in market leverage.[7] But book leverage is unaffected by stock price changes – and it also falls. Thus, the debt issues must be the primary driver of this observed increase in leverage. This substantial increase in debt following the SEO is inconsistent both with the Market Timing

Theory and the more extreme versions of the Pecking Order Theory. Both presume that firms have no leverage target, and firms thus have no reason to readjust leverage following their SEOs.

Offering Size and Leverage Rebalancing. A company facing large capital requirements should adjust both its debt and equity; because a larger equity offering will move the firm's leverage further below its target level, future debt issues must be larger to rebalance leverage. Thus, Strategic Financial Management implies that the larger the size of an SEO, the larger the debt issues that should follow it.

To test this rebalancing hypothesis, BFS employ the average market leverage of the SEO firm during quarters -12 to -5 as a proxy for target leverage. Consistent with the rebalancing hypothesis, they find that the SEO firms leverage is below the proxy for target leverage at the end of the offering quarter. The average difference between market leverage and the firm's historical average leverage in the offering quarter is -3.2% – this difference is statistically significant. (Employing data on book leverage yields similar results.)

Because leverage of SEO firms is below target after the SEO, the rebalancing hypothesis implies that firms have incentives to increase debt after the offering to rebalance their capital structures. BFS run Fama-MacBeth regressions to examine whether the relative size of debt issues following the SEO can be explained by firms' estimated deviation from target leverage.[8] Consistent with this rebalancing hypothesis, they find that the coefficients of the deviation variables are negative and statistically significant. Their estimates imply that firms whose SEOs push leverage further below their target level issue more debt in the periods following the SEOs.

7.4.4   SEOs by growth versus value firms

A firm's investment opportunities have a profound effect on an array of corporate policy choices (see Smith and Watts, 1992). But perhaps its most important impact is on a firm's choice of its leverage target. As we discussed in Chapter 6, because they are more concerned with Underinvestment Problems, growth firms use less debt than value (assets in place) firms. Also, value firms have more collateral and face greater pressure from investors to use debt to control Free Cash-Flow (Overinvestment) Problems. If the purpose of the SEO is to raise capital to finance a large investment project by a growth firm, an increasing stock price prior to the offering will cause market leverage to be, not just low, but also falling as the SEO approaches. After the offering the firm's debt capacity increases from the exercise of its growth options and their transformation into assets in place. As debt is issued to complete the financing of the project, leverage rises. Conversely, a value company – with more internally generated cash, higher target leverage, and typically smaller investment projects – is more likely to use part of its SEO proceeds to pay down its outstanding debt. Thus, a value firm's leverage falls at the SEO both because new equity is sold and part of its debt is repaid. These transactions thus replenish the firm's unused debt capacity.

Based on the firm's market-to-book ratio, BFS identify these two firm types at the end of the year before the SEO for the industrial firms in their sample. The issuing firm is classified as a growth firm if its market-to-book ratio is in the upper third of COMPUSTAT firms in that year – if it is in the lower third, it is classified as a value firm. Employing this process, 69% of their industrial SEO firms are classified as growth firms and 10% as value firms.

As their analysis suggests, their growth firms' leverage is significantly lower than that of their value firms. For the 12 quarters before their offering, the average leverage of their growth firms falls – this fall is caused by their rising stock prices over this period. Reflecting the influx of new equity from the SEO, leverage falls further in the offering quarter. But average leverage then increases, attaining its pre-offering level within several quarters, and continues to increase over the entire 20 post-offering quarters in their data.

In contrast, the average leverage for their value firms increased until a few quarters before the offering. As the SEO nears, leverage begins to fall. With the equity infusion, it falls further in the SEO quarter. It then begins to rise, but over the 20 post-SEO quarters, it never attains its level before the offering. This finding suggests that rebalancing its capital structure is a more important consideration for value firms than for growth firms. Consistent with this observation, value firms tended to have weaker financial ratios than those of the median firm in their industry prior to their offerings; moreover, their financial condition is deteriorating. During this pre-offering period, the financial ratios of growth firms are stronger and improving.

7.4.5   SEOs by regulated versus unregulated firms

Although frequently excluded from empirical corporate finance analyses, BFS compare SEOs by regulated utilities with those of unregulated industrial firms. They suggest that in the examination of these questions, regulated utilities merit special attention for three reasons. Compared to unregulated industrials: (1) the market values of utilities primarily reflect that of their long-lived tangible assets and thus Underinvestment Problems associated with debt should be lower, (2) the regulatory process limits managerial discretion and hence Free Cash-Flow Problems should be better controlled, and (3) the public hearings and mandated disclosures that are part of the regulatory process, information asymmetries between investors and managers should be smaller. These differences lower the costs of SEOs for utilities and thus should lead to observable differences in financial policy choices between utility and industrial SEOs.

Offering Size. With lower total issuance costs, the optimal SEO size for a utility should be smaller than for the typical industrial firm. The data in Table 7.1 indicate that proceeds of the typical utility SEO are 5.0% of its enterprise value, substantially less than the 18.7% for the typical industrial. Furthermore, the typical utility SEO sells 12.8% of shares outstanding compared to 20.8% for the typical industrial.

Regulation, Leverage, and Investment Spending. Because of its greater debt capacity, a utility requires a larger investment project to trigger an SEO. BFS report that the increase in investment spending around utility SEOs is larger than for industrial SEOs. Also, the market leverage of utilities is substantially higher for the typical utility SEO firm than for the typical industrial SEO firm (close to .45 compared to around .20 in the 12 quarters proceeding the SEO and the 20 quarters after the SEO). It is also higher than for the typical value industrial firm as well (average leverage for their value firms is between .30 and .37 over the corresponding period).

7.4.6   Stock price changes around SEOs

BFS also examine stock prices around offering announcements for both their growth and value firms. In the three days around their announcements, growth firms have slightly more negative CARs than value firms: -2.4% versus -2.0%. However, those firms that are undertaking larger investment projects have significantly less negative CARs than those with smaller projects: -1.82% versus -2.7%. (Jung, Kim and Stulz, 1996 also find that SEO firms undertaking larger projects have less negative stock price reactions to SEO announcements.) But over the six months preceding the offering announcements, growth firms have larger stock price increases than value firms: 45% versus 30.7%. And those firms undertaking larger projects also had larger CARs: 41.5% versus 32.7%.

These observations provide a potential resolution for bothersome results from prior studies of SEOs. Since an SEO is a voluntary transaction and thus presumably a value-increasing decision, why would the stock price fall at its announcement? We think that three facts can, together, help explain this observation. First, the typical new investment project is a valuable corporate asset – this is reflected in the double-digit abnormal returns over the six months preceding the SEO. Second, external investors have limited information about the entire project. Presumably, it would be an even better project if it could be financed just using the firm's current resources – its cash balances, the unborrowed balance on its line of credit, and the cash flows from its other projects, along with cash flows this project might generate. Third, if the firm announces an SEO, these currently available resources are clearly insufficient to finance the project; this is bad news. But this "bad news" should be kept in context. The project that it is financing is an extremely valuable project – just not as valuable as it might have been if the SEO were not required.

7.5 Summary

After reviewing the process by which public firms raise additional equity, we review the costs associated with these seasoned equity offerings (SEOs). These costs are much higher than those of raising external debt. For this reason, public firms are rarely at their target leverage.

Most discussions of corporate financing policy are based on either the Tradeoff Theory or the Pecking Order Theory, which assume that the primary impetus for SEOs is that their leverage is too high – that the firm has reached its debt capacity. But the evidence presented by Barclay, Fu and Smith (2021) reveals that the typical SEO firm's leverage is below its target level and thus well below its debt capacity. They present an alternative theory, Strategic Financial Management, that retains the productive aspects of the other major theories but avoids their major problems.

According to this theory, the decision to issue equity, rather than debt, is motivated by a large investment opportunity. Managers consider not only the near-term capital requirements for this investment, but the longer-term requirements, as well – they are forward looking. If the external financing for the project were just to employ debt, then prior to project completion the firm would exceed its debt capacity. Thus, at some time during the implementation of the project, the firm will have to have an SEO to avoid exceeding its debt capacity. BFS suggest that in such circumstances its first external security sale should be an SEO. The funding for the remainder of the project will be debt. This early equity infusion lowers the firm's leverage and thus better controls the Underinvestment Problem. Subsequent debt financing moves the firm back toward its target leverage.

From an examination of their evidence of over 8,000 SEOs these conclusions follow: (1) Over the three years prior to the SEO, leverage is below target and falling due to stock price increases for the typical SEO firm; leverage falls further due to the equity infusion from the SEO. (2) For the typical SEO firm, the level of corporate investment spending increases substantially in the SEO quarter, and it remains high throughout the five-year period post-SEO. (3) For the majority of SEO issuers, the increase in investment in the three years following the SEO exceeded the offering proceeds. (4) For the five-year period following the SEO, leverage increases primarily because of debt issues. (5) BFS classify 69% of SEO issuers as growth firms, whose average market-to-book asset ratio is above 2.5, while 10 % were classified as value companies whose ratios average just above 1.0. (6) Project financing appears to be the primary motive for SEOs by growth firms; lowering leverage appears to be more important for value firms. (7) Regulated firms have smaller information disparities between managers and investors; they have smaller asymmetric information-based costs; they have smaller SEOs than unregulated firms. (8) Over the six months preceding their SEOs growth firms' abnormal stock price returns are 45%; it is 31% for value firms. At SEO announcement, growth firms have a -2.4% abnormal stock price reaction, for value firms it averages -2.0%.

Notes

1. This section contains material that has been revised and updated from Smith (1986a and 1986b).
2. The term seasoned equity offering (SEO) is used when the firm already has publicly traded shares. When a firm offers publicly traded equity for the first time, the offering is called an *initial public offering* (IPO). Our focus in this chapter is on SEOs.
3. A road show consists of presentations by senior management (often with the aid of the underwriters) to market the upcoming offering. The typical attendants include institutional investors, representatives from brokerage firms, and money managers, among others.
4. This section draws on the material in Barclay, Fu and Smith (2021) and Fu and Smith (2021).
5. BFS divide industrial firms into three sub-groups: Value firms if their market-to-book ratio falls in the bottom third of COMPUSTAT industrial firms in that year; growth firms if they are in the highest third; remaining firms are in the middle group.
6. Although our discussion thus far presumes that the firm's leverage target is constant over time, this typically is an oversimplification. The development of major growth opportunities reduces the firm's target leverage – the debt capacity of growth options is negative (see Barclay, Morellec and Smith, 2006).
7. This average abnormal return is potentially biased: (1) the fall in leverage in the two quarters prior to and in the SEO quarter reduce the risk of the firm's equity, and (2) as the firm's growth options are exercised the company's asset risk is reduced. For both reasons, the normal return for the shares is overstated.
8. Most prior studies of capital structure use either cross-sectional or panel regressions and thus ignore the correlation of regression residuals across firms. Cross-correlation causes standard errors of average slopes to be understated and significance overstated. Because there is some clustering of SEOs in various periods, this can be a problem. Fama-MacBeth standard errors account for this potential problem.

8   Corporate payout policy

Corporate payout policy addresses two basic questions: (1) how much cash to distribute to shareholders (if any) and (2) whether the cash should be distributed through dividends and/or share repurchases.[1] This chapter summarizes the theory and evidence related to these important questions.

8.1   A few basic facts

Corporations distribute significant amounts of cash to shareholders. According to Barron's, global dividends hit an all-time high of $1.4 trillion in 2019.[2] And S&P 500 companies were "on track" to buy back $940 billion of stock in 2019, according to Goldman Sachs.[3]

The propensity to pay dividends is highest among larger, more profitable industrial companies and banks, which are noted for making particularly high and consistent dividend payouts (Denis and Osobov, 2008; Floyd, Li and Skinner, 2015). Many firms, however, neither pay cash dividends nor repurchase shares. In 2017, it is estimated that 58% of U.S. nonfinancial corporations did not pay dividends, while 52% did not repurchase stock; on average, in each year over the period 2011 to 2017, 42.1% of nonfinancial firms paid neither dividends nor repurchased shares, while 23.4% both paid dividends and repurchased stock (Brealey, Myers and Allen, 2020, pp. 426–427). Although some non-dividend paying firms are in financial distress, many are growth firms, which use retained earnings to finance investment. For instance, Amazon.com – a firm clearly not in financial distress – as of 2021, has never paid a dividend to its shareholders.

Figure 8.1 from Zeng and Luk (2020) displays the trends in dividends and share repurchases by listed firms covered by COMPUSTAT over the period 1980 through 2018. Between 1980 to 2002, there is a relatively constant and steep decline in the percentage of firms that pay cash dividends. However, over this same time, total dividend payouts to investors increase (in both real and nominal terms). This difference in trends is explained by the fact that the reduction in firms paying dividends is driven largely by firms that have paid very small dividends in the first place and by an increase in new firms that have not initiated dividend payments. The higher dividends that are paid by large, profitable firms "swamped the modest dividend reductions from the loss of many small players" (DeAngelo, DeAngelo and Skinner, 2004).

Stock repurchases are rare in 1980 but increase significantly over the succeeding years. After 1996, total payouts that are made through repurchases exceed those made through dividends in most years. In the aftermath of recessions in the U.S. economy – the first years of the 21st century and 2009–2010 – firms reduce their total payouts to shareholders. During these years, firms are more likely to maintain their regular cash dividends but make large cuts in stock repurchases.

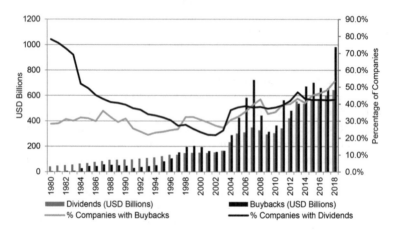

Figure 8.1   Trends in dividends and stock repurchases (1980–2018)

This figure displays the total cash paid to shareholders through dividends and stock repurchases from 1980 through 2018. Also displayed are the percentages of companies in each year that paid dividends and repurchased stock. Only listed firms with fundamental data on S&P's Computstat database are included. Dividend and repurchase data may include the amount paid on preferred shares. *Source:* This figure was originally published in Zeng and Luk (2020), S&P Dow Jones Indices (permission to republish).

Tax codes and regulations, which potentially affect payout decisions, vary across countries. Denis and Osobov (2008) present evidence on the international trends in dividend payouts over the 1989–2002 period. Their evidence reveals that there are common determinants of dividends across countries. In particular, they find that large, profitable firms are more likely to pay dividends in all six countries that they study (United States, Canada, United Kingdom, Germany, France, and Japan).

8.2   Payout policy – M&M Irrelevance Proposition revisited

As discussed in Chapter 3, serious scholarly analysis of corporate payout policy began with Miller and Modigliani (1961). They show that, assuming a perfect capital market and holding investment policy fixed (or at least independent of payout policy), neither the amount nor form of the payout (dividends versus share repurchases) affect firm value. Under these stringent assumptions, corporate payout policy is irrelevant. You will recall from Chapter 3 that a perfect capital market has the following characteristics:

- There are no taxes on either firms or investors.
- There are no contacting, transactions, information, bankruptcy, or agency costs.
- All market participants are price takers – no firm nor investor can individually change the way securities are priced by the market.

The intuition behind the *M&M Dividend Irrelevance Proposition* can be illustrated through a simple example. Suppose that ABC Corp. is an all-equity firm with 100 shares outstanding, and it has made an investment. Suppose also that this project is the firm's only asset; it will result in a net cash flow of $1,100 one year from now; and ABC will dissolve at the end of the year. Assume also that investors can buy and sell shares in the marketplace without transaction costs or taxes and all participants in the market share in the same information. If shareholders require a 10% rate of return to hold the stock, the current value of ABC is $1,100/1.1 = $1,000 or $10 per share.

One option ABC has is to pay no dividend in the current period and an $11 liquidating dividend per share in one year. Investors who prefer cash now can create "homemade dividends" simply by selling some of their shares. Others preferring higher payouts in the future can refrain from selling their shares. The firm could sell new shares to pay dividends to existing shareholders in the current period. However, this will not change total firm value since any feasible pattern of dividends can be achieved by shareholders on their own through the buying and selling of shares in the marketplace.[4]

The form of its payouts also does not affect ABC's value. For example, at the end of the year it does not matter if shareholders receive an $11 per share liquidating dividend or if they receive $11 per share through a share repurchase – cash is cash. With a fixed investment policy, firm value within a perfect market is determined by the present value of the firm's future net cash flows, not by the firm's payout policy.

For simplicity, this example focuses on an all-equity firm with no uncertainty about cash flows. But the same result is easily demonstrated in the case of a leveraged firm with a fixed amount of debt in its capital structure and where there is uncertainty about future cash flows.

As in Chapter 3, the M&M Dividend Irrelevance Proposition implies that if payout policy is to matter it must be due either to a violation of one or more of the perfect market assumptions or because investment and payout policies are interdependent. Below we discuss the implications of relaxing these conditions and the related empirical research.

8.3   Taxes

The returns to common stock investors come in two forms: capital gains – selling a stock for more than its original purchase price – and dividends. While the relative tax rates on capital gains and dividends have varied significantly over time in the United States, the tax rates for individual investors have generally been higher on dividends. In addition, investors can reduce the effective tax rate on capital gains by deferring the sales of stocks that have appreciated (since taxes on capital gains are paid only when realized).[5]

Taxes clearly affect bond pricing – tax-free municipal bonds sell at lower promised pre-tax yields than taxable federal government bonds (holding risk and time to maturity constant). Correspondingly, some economists have argued that the pre-tax expected returns should increase with the dividend yield.[6] The higher expected returns compensate investors for the increased taxes they have to pay when they receive their returns in the form of dividends.

Although most individuals face higher taxes on dividends than capital gains, it is important to note that tax exposures vary. Non-profit institutions – for example, most universities, charitable organizations, or religious institutions – are tax exempt, paying taxes on neither dividends nor capital gains. Some investors also are indifferent between dividends and capital gains – for example, assets in pension funds or individual retirement accounts are untaxed until withdrawal, when the amount withdrawn is taxed at ordinary tax rates. Corporations historically have paid lower taxes on dividends. Finally, some international investors receive quite favorable tax treatment of dividends – for example, the Japanese tax code sets the rate on dividends at zero. In addition, regulation constrains some investors. For instance, some financial institutions are legally restricted from holding stocks that have no historic record of paying dividends. Other investors – for example, retirees who prefer a steady source of income from dividends, rather than having to finance consumption through periodic stock sales – prefer high steady dividend payments.

The fact that investors vary in their preferences for dividends has led some economists to argue that the pre-tax expected returns on stocks will not depend on dividend yields. Certain clienteles might favor low dividend paying stocks, while others prefer high dividend paying stocks. However, given the array of dividend preferences among various investors, corporations are unlikely to be able to increase their stock prices by shifting the form of their payouts between dividends and share repurchase. Were that possible, competition for lower costs of capital among firms suggests that they already would have done so.

Over the years, there has been a great deal of empirical research that attempts to determine whether taxes affect pre-tax expected stock returns (that is, the stock price).[7] These results are quite mixed and, taken together, are inconclusive. Also, empirical studies suggest that changes in the tax code have not been the driving force behind the increased use of share repurchases in recent decades (Floyd, Li and Skinner, 2015). Many firms continue to pay high dividends, despite their potential tax disadvantages for some investors.[8] In fact, many U.S. firms paid substantial dividends in the 1960s and 1970s when top-bracket tax rates on dividends never fell below 70%. While it is difficult to draw definitive conclusions, it is relatively safe to say that there is no compelling evidence that differences in tax rates on dividends versus capital gains play major roles in affecting corporate payout policies or stock prices.

8.4 Free cash flow

In addition to no taxes, the M&M Irrelevance Proposition assumes there are no information, contracting, or agency costs, and investment policy is independent of payout policy. These assumptions clearly are violated in actual markets, and so firm value might be affected by a firm's payout policy working through one of these channels.

As we discussed in Chapter 5, *Free Cash Flow (FCF)* is cash flow in excess of that required to fund available positive net present value (NPV) projects. Firm value maximization dictates that FCF be paid out to shareholders (which would allow them to invest in other firms with positive NPV projects).[9] But as we have argued, managers, as agents of the shareholders, can have incentives to use FCF to grow a firm beyond its optimal size: managerial compensation tends to increase with firm size; they might gain prestige from managing a larger firm; and using funds to invest in "pet projects" can increase a manager's personal utility. As a direct implication of the definition of FCF, firm value is destroyed if managers retain it. This agency problem is of particular concern within established value firms – firms with what Myers calls assets in place – that generate large amounts of cash but have limited profitable investment opportunities. Because investment opportunities are not readily observable (information is asymmetric), it is difficult for external investors to monitor whether or not the firm has FCF.

8.4.1 Control of the Free Cash Flow Problem

As we discuss in Chapter 5, Jensen argues that debt contracts commit the firm to pay cash to debtholders. Cash payments to outside claimants reduce the firm's FCF and provide increased incentives to managers to work harder to avoid default and bankruptcy. But unlike interest payments on debt, dividend payments are discretionary – thus exposing the managers to a potentially less binding constraint. Prior research going back to Lintner (1956), however, strongly suggests that managers are quite reluctant to cut regular dividend payments (see also Brav, Graham, Harvey and Michaely, 2005). Thus, an increase in the firm's regular dividend, although not as strong a commitment as that with a bond issue, still provides a reasonably credible commitment that managers will continue to make the higher cash payouts in the future. Thus, higher regular dividend payments can potentially reduce agency costs by providing better control of the FCF problem – both by reducing shareholder monitoring costs as well as by reducing the residual losses from investments in negative NPV projects.

FCF also can be distributed to shareholders through share repurchases and specially designated dividends, for example, an "extra" dividend (Brickley, 1983). However, managers have more flexibility to reduce these payments over future periods than in the case of regular dividends. (In terms of commitment, share repurchases are like dating, interest payments are more like being married.) Ultimately, there is a spectrum in levels of commitment with these mechanisms for distributing free cash flow: at the high end are long-term debt contracts, followed by short-term debt, ordinary dividends, share repurchases, and finally specially designated dividends.

Existing agency cost explanations for firm payout policies vary somewhat in motivation and focus, but most are based on some type of informational asymmetry problem. For example, both Rozeff (1982) and Easterbrook (1984) argue that higher dividends reduce the resources under managers' control, thus limiting their ability to make wasteful investments (although they use different language, they basically are arguing that higher dividends can help to control the Free Cash Flow Problem). By forcing managers to raise capital for new projects in external markets, it exposes managers to greater discipline by the capital market. Managers who consider funding a negative NPV project will find it difficult, if not impossible, to raise money in external markets – they will have to pay higher prices to obtain these funds. Although a commitment to pay out more cash to shareholders reduces the agency costs associated with FCF, it increases other costs by forcing the firm to use external capital markets more frequently (Myers and Majluf, 1984). But there is an attendant longer-term benefit in doing so. As we noted in Chapter 7, a component of a firm-commitment underwritten equity offering is the due diligence process. Establishing a corporate payout policy that forces a firm to return to external capital markets periodically, requiring it to go through this due diligence process, subjects the firm to periodic, intense, sophisticated oversight. Three things should be noted: (1) Because Non-Disclosure Agreements (NDAs) have been signed by all the relevant parties – importantly including the lead investment bank – the investment bank can examine proprietary as well as public information prior to recommending an investment in the firm's equity offering to its best customers. (2) Under U.S. securities laws, it is illegal to hire an investment bank to "tout" the firm's stock. (3) Investment banks perform similar services for their entire array of clients. Their ability to attract new business and retain existing clients depends critically on their reputation for competent investigation, thoughtful evaluation, and accurate certification. These reputations are built over a long period of time – such reputations are built by the teaspoon but lost by the bucket. Therefore, a top-tier investment bank will guard the value of its reputational capital vigorously. In summary, having credible investment banks underwrite an offering helps to bond managerial commitments that the funds will be used for value-increasing projects and activities.[10]

8.4.2 Interaction between payout and financing policies

Younger growth firms generate little FCF. They often will make no cash payouts to shareholders, using available cash balances, internally generated cash, and draws against their line of credit to fund new investment projects. But the flow of new growth opportunities often exceeds these sources of funds. As we discussed in Chapter 7, when either leverage nears the firm's debt capacity or a large growth opportunity is developed that would cause the firm to exceed its debt capacity, the firm will need to raise equity capital. Even with no payouts, a young, fast-growing firm may have an equity offering every two or three years.

In contrast, mature firms producing substantial amounts of free cash flow and generating more limited growth options typically adopt higher payout policies that require them to hire an investment bank and return to equity markets less frequently (typically every eight to 12 years). Such a firm could, at least in principle, retain funds within the firm to finance its activities and avoid the costs of accessing external capital markets. However, there is a longer-term cost to such a strategy – the increased likelihood of value-decreasing investments. By committing to periodic equity offerings that are underwritten by credible investment banks, managers help to assure investors that they will not waste funds on value-decreasing investments and activities. Despite the fact that this strategy involves costs, it is often the value-maximizing strategy – the benefits exceed its costs.

8.4.3   Empirical evidence

Overall, the empirical evidence appears to support the agency-related predictions on corporate payout policy. In contrast to demand-side considerations, such as those based on investor tax clienteles, the FCF framework appears to explain the "broad brush features of observed payout policies" relatively well (DeAngelo, DeAngelo and Skinner, 2007; Denis and Osobov, 2008).[11] Consistent with their *Life-Cycle Theory*, DeAngelo, DeAngelo and Stulz (2006) document that that "the fraction of publicly traded industrial firms that pay dividends is high when retained earnings are a large fraction of total equity (and total assets) and falls to near zero when most of the equity is contributed rather than earned."[12] They "conservatively estimate" that had the 25 largest long-standing dividend-paying companies in their sample in 2002 not paid dividends over the 1950–2002 period their cash balances would have totaled $1.8 trillion (51% of total assets), up from $160 billion. With relatively low leverage and huge cash balances, managers would have had many opportunities to make investments and adopt policies that benefitted themselves at the expense of shareholders. Consistent payment of dividends limited these opportunities.

8.5   Informational content of dividends

Miller and Modigliani (1961) were well aware of the fact that the stock market generally reacts positively (negatively) to dividend increases (decreases) – sometimes spectacularly so.[13] Numerous researchers have studied the stock market reactions to announced dividend changes. On average, announcements of increases in dividends and initiations of dividends are met with an "immediate" and significant stock price increase of about 1% and 3%, respectively, while announcements of dividend cuts and omissions are met on average with a 6% to 10% decline (DeAngelo, DeAngelo and Skinner, 2007, p. 182). M&M argue that "such a phenomenon is not inconsistent with irrelevance to the extent that it is merely a reflection of what might be called the 'informational content' of dividends." In actual markets, in contrast to their model's assumptions, stock markets are unlikely to be strong-form efficient. As such, dividend changes have the potential to convey private information held by managers to outside investors.

The foundation underlying the informational content of dividends is found in Lintner (1956). Lintner's interviews of corporate managers led to several conclusions, which have been reaffirmed in subsequent surveys (e.g., Brav, Graham, Harvey and Michaely, 2005). In particular, managers are reluctant to reduce regular dividend payments, and in turn raise the dividend only when they believe that the firm will have sufficient earnings to maintain the higher level in the future. Accordingly, outside investors infer inside information about the prospects of the firm from the announcements of dividend changes.

This line of reasoning suggests that dividend changes should be reliable signals of future earnings and cash flows. Researchers have found that dividend changes tend to be correlated with current period earnings, which are often announced simultaneously. However, they have found little support for the hypothesis that dividend changes convey information about future changes in earnings or cash flows (see DeAngelo, DeAngelo and Skinner, 2007, for a summary of the relevant research). So, it is unclear what information is being conveyed to the market by dividend changes. A recent paper by Michaely, Rossi and Weber (2021) provides a potential solution to this puzzle. They find that dividend changes convey information about the future volatility of future cash flows (as opposed to information about the level of cash flows or discount rates). Dividend increases tend be followed by less volatility, while the opposite is true for dividend decreases.[14]

Corporate managers are less reluctant to cut share repurchases than dividends. Thus, an increase in share repurchases should presumably convey less information to the market than dividend increases. Nevertheless, the stock market generally greets announcements of stock repurchases positively. Comment and Jarrell (1991) find that announcements of open-market share repurchase programs are associated with an average abnormal return of about 2% and that the size of the announcement period return increases with the number of shares sought. Dann (1981) documents average stock returns of approximately 15% within one day of the announcements of large intrafirm tender offers (median firm in his sample sought to buy back more than 10% of its outstanding shares). No other class of security holders (e.g., bondholders) experiences a systematic decline in value around these announcements – suggesting that on average the announcement of an intrafirm tender offer generates an increase in overall firm value. Michaely, Rossi and Weber (2021) provide evidence that similar to dividend increases, share repurchases convey information to the market about the volatility of future cash flows. In both cases, the magnitude of the effect increases with the size of the payout.

8.6   Conclusions

A substantial body of theoretical and empirical work on corporate payout policy now exists. While there are aspects of payout policy that are still not well understood, several conclusions can be drawn:

- While tax considerations and personal preferences may lead some investors to prefer high or low dividend paying stocks, it is unlikely that a firm can increase its value simply by changing the form of the payout from dividends to repurchases or vice versa.
- Value maximization implies that surplus cash (free cash flow – FCF) should be paid out to investors. Dividends are one method for committing to paying out cash to shareholders. Managers appear reluctant to increase the regular dividend unless they are confident that they can maintain it in the future. Managers have more flexibility to vary cash payouts when they use specially designated dividends or share repurchases.
- Very few firms repurchased shares in 1980. Cash payouts to shareholders were made almost entirely by dividends. Since then, there has been a marked increase in share repurchases. Cash distributed through repurchases by U.S. firms in recent years exceeds dividend payments. However, this increase in share repurchases does not appear to be driven by changes in the tax code.
- A commitment to pay out more cash to shareholders through higher regular dividends reduces the agency costs associated with FCF, but it also increases costs by forcing the firm to use external capital markets more frequently when they have positive NPV projects in which to

invest (Myers and Majluf, 1984). This tradeoff helps to explain why the observed level and possibly the form of cash payouts tends to vary over the "life-cycle" of a firm. Younger growth firms often make little or no cash payouts to shareholders and use internally generated cash and the proceeds from SEOs to fund new investment projects. As the firm matures, it is more likely to generate excess cash and will begin to repurchase shares. Older firms with limited investment opportunities and more predictable/stable cash flows tend to pay higher regular dividends, possibly coupled with share repurchases (in recent years, over 20% of U.S. firms both paid dividends and repurchased shares).

- Corporate payouts increase the frequency of external equity sales. Although these SEOs are expensive, they expose the firm to intense monitoring by sophisticated investment bankers, whose value in the marketplace depends on maintaining a reputation for effective oversight and monitoring. After signing an NDA, the underwriters have access to both public and non-public information prior to recommending the shares to their customers. Even with no payouts, growth firms with growth options but little internally generated cash return to equity markets frequently, every three to five years. Older more mature firms return less frequently, every eight to 12 years.

- Dividend changes tend to convey inside information to outside investors that cause significant changes in stock price. It is not entirely clear what the exact nature of this information is, but recent evidence suggests that dividend changes convey information to the market about future cash flow volatility.

Notes

1. Dividends include regular dividends and specially designated dividends (e.g., an "extra" dividend). Shares can be repurchased through open-market purchases, intrafirm tender offers, or targeted share repurchases (for example, from a large blockholder).
2. Strauss, Lawrence C., "Global dividends hit a record $1.4 trillion in 2019. Their growth rate slowed, however," Barron's, February 17, 2020. https://www.barrons.com/articles/global-dividend-payouts-hit-a-record-in-2019-and-80-of-u-s-companies-increased-their-dividends-51581944402?mod=article_signInButton
3. Egan, Matt, "Stock buybacks are reaching dangerous levels," CNN Business (July 30, 2019). https://www.cnn.com/2019/07/30/investing/stock-buybacks-debt-leverage

4. For example, let's examine two policies. First, ABC could sell 100 additional shares at $5/share to pay a $5 per share dividend to current shareholders. Each of the 200 shares (100 original shares plus the 100 new shares), which would be priced by the marketplace at $5/share, would receive a dividend of $1,100/200 = $5.50 at the end of the year. The buyers of the 100 additional shares receive the necessary 10% return to motivate them to purchase the stock at $5/share. Conversely, an investor wanting to maximize the payout at the end of the year could use their $5 dividend to purchase additional shares of stock in the firm. Second, if ABC paid no current dividend, an investor desiring a $5 per share dividend could achieve it by selling half of their shares at $10/share. Note that it does not matter if the firm issues a $5 dividend to existing shareholders in the current period or uses the proceeds from a stock sale to repurchase 50 of their 100 shares. The firm could sell 50 shares to new investors at a price of $10/share and use the proceeds to repurchase 50 shares from existing shareholders. The resulting number of shares remains at 100 and each share is paid a liquidating dividend of $11 in one year for a 10% return on the current stock price of $10 per share. The payoff to existing shareholders is the same as under the $5 dividend option. They collectively receive a total payout of $500 in the current and $550 in total payout in one year under either payout method.

5. Under the current tax code (June 2021), an unrealized capital gain postponed into one's estate disappears altogether because of the "step up in basis" that occurs at death.

6. For example, Brennan (1970) derives a capital asset pricing model in which expected returns on a stock are linearly and positively related to both its beta (systematic risk) and its dividend yield (dividend/stock price).

7. Kalay and Lemmon (2008) provide a detailed review of this research.

8. There may be costs associated with share repurchases that help to offset their potential tax advantages. Barclay and Smith (1988) argue that open-market repurchase programs provide managers with opportunities to use inside information to benefit themselves at the stockholders' expense. They find that the bid-ask spreads widen around repurchase announcements, which is predicted by their analysis.

9. If the firm is overly levered, it should use the FCF to reduce its debt.

10. This certification function that an investment bank provides is not unique. Independent directors, corporate law firms, public accounting firms, commercial banks, and bond rating agencies all engage in various forms of monitoring the firm, and the distribution of their public reports are a form of bonding. Each of these groups represent a corporate expense. But it would be short-sighted of a firm to focus on these costs without at the same time considering their benefits. The firm ultimately should assemble a collection of external bonding agencies that provide public investors with the confidence to invest in the firm's securities.

11. Agency problems between shareholders and bondholders can also affect a firm's payout policy, e.g., covenants in debt contracts frequently limit the amount of cash that can be paid to the firm's shareholders. We discuss these concerns elsewhere in this book.

12. The authors argue that the proportion of total equity and of total assets that is earned versus contributed (for example, through stock offerings) is a "logical proxy for the life-cycle stage a firm currently finds itself because it measures the extent to which the firm is self-financing or reliant on external capital."

13. Miller frequently told a story about when he was giving a lecture to the research department of a large Wall Street investment firm. During his talk on *dividend-policy irrelevancy*, there was an announcement that AT&T had just increased its dividend from the level it had maintained for many years. Within a short period of time, AT&T's stock priced at increased in price by over 10%.

14. The analysis in this paper does not explain why the stock market values information on cash-flow volatility. The authors provide evidence that firm cash-flow volatility around dividend events reflects at least in part a systematic component. However, we remain far from a comfortable understanding of this result. For example, our analysis in Chapter 3 would lead to the opposite conclusion from what these authors document. Given its option-like payoffs, a reduction in volatility would be expected to reduce the value of a levered firm's equity.

9 Managerial insights and concluding comments

This book provides an advanced introduction to modern corporate finance, an academic field that has been developing over the past six decades through significant theoretical and empirical research. While there are still unresolved issues and questions, great progress has been made. The topics and concepts presented in this book are now a central component of the curriculum of virtually all business schools. They are relevant not just for managers in financial functions, but for all managers, given the increasing use of cross-functional teams within firms. To be a productive member of these teams, a manager must have a basic understanding of all major functions within the firm, not just an understanding of their particular specialty.

Corporate finance is broadly concerned with three major decisions: (1) the choice of projects in which to invest – *capital budgeting*, (2) the choice of how to finance the firm's investments and operations – *capital structure/financing policy*, and (3) the choice of both the size and the form (dividends or share repurchases) of distributions to the firm's shareholders – *payout policy*. In this chapter, we conclude this book by summarizing key insights and managerial implications related each of these policies.

9.1 Capital budgeting

Investors vary substantially in both wealth and risk aversion, but they commonly share the same objective – wanting professional managers to maximize firm value. Simply stated, firm value increases by investing in projects that are worth more than their cost. While easy to say, the practical question is: *How do managers determine whether the benefits of an investment are greater than its costs, given that projects vary in both risk as well as the timing of their expected cash flows?* The solution to this complex problem, already commonly used among today's financial managers, is *Net Present Value* (NPV) analysis.

NPV analysis involves discounting future expected cash flows from a project to their present (current) value. The basic idea behind NPV analysis is simple – a dollar today is worth more than a dollar tomorrow. And since investors are risk averse, it is important to use a discount rate appropriate for the risk of the project. Many financial managers employ a *Weighted Average Cost of Capital* (WACC) for all potential projects; this is a discount rate that reflects the average cost of capital for the firm's existing projects. Some variant of the *Capital Asset Pricing Model* often is used to estimate the cost of equity capital. But employing a single WACC for all projects can lead to underinvestment in projects that have low project-specific risks and overinvestment in high-risk projects. Managers should adjust the discount rate when they are considering projects that differ substantially in risk from their firm's typical investments.

Many potential investments contain valuable embedded options – options to time additional investments, the option to abandon an unsuccessful project, and options to expand a successful project. A variant of the *Black-Scholes Model* is used by some firms to value these *real options* quantitatively. However, others employ the model on a more qualitative basis.

The *Efficient Markets Hypothesis* is among the most tested in all the social sciences. The research suggests that managers generally should trust market prices. Those in charge of their firm's securities portfolio, exchange-rate policy, commodity purchases, and so on should avoid speculative positions based on personal forecasts of security prices, interest rates, exchange rates, or commodity prices. Managers are unlikely to beat the market by engaging in speculative trading, and such trading can impose significant risks on the firm. Rather, they should concentrate on developing, financing, and implementing profitable investment opportunities.

Of critical importance is that there be a close link between strategy and corporate finance. Investment decisions need to be made within the context of the firm's specific strategy. Today's CFOs are spending more time than in the past on strategy development and implementation – they bring important financial skills and tools to bear on the planning process.

9.2   Capital structure

Simply cast, the financing problem comes down to the question of how much equity capital should the firm raise versus borrowing? Modigliani and Miller (1958) initiated serious research on this question. They rigorously demonstrate that the leverage decision does not affect firm value in a perfect capital market with investment policy held fixed. Actual capital markets, however, are not perfect, and significant subsequent research has been conducted on how market imperfections and interactions between financing and investment policies might affect firm value.

The basic *Tradeoff Theory* argues there are both costs and benefits of debt financing. The potential costs of debt are the direct and indirect costs of financial distress including Underinvestment Problems. The potential benefits of debt come from corporate tax savings and mitigation of the Overinvestment (Free Cash Flow) Problem. According to the Tradeoff Theory, depending on such things as the firm's marginal tax rate and investment opportunity set, there is an optimal target capital structure, toward which the firm adjusts over time. Random events, such as a change in the firm's market value, can move a firm away from its target capital structure. But since there are costs in adjusting, this adjustment is not immediate but occurs over time – for example, as the firm obtains additional financing from external capital markets.

The empirical evidence suggests that, for the typical firm, corporate taxes are at best a secondary consideration in the leverage decisions. Apparently more important are agency-related concerns and transaction costs. Excessive debt within capital structures of growth firms can create incentives for managers to underinvest in positive NPV projects. Growth firms, whose value largely reflects that of its intangible assets, thus bear higher costs when excessive debt claims place them in financial distress. These firms thus set leverage targets lower. In contrast, firms whose value primarily reflects that of its long-lived tangible assets in place tend to set their leverage targets higher for at least two reasons. First, they often generate free cash flow (cash flow beyond that needed to fund available positive NPV projects). Debt claims require the managers to pay this cash to investors, rather than to invest it in negative NPV projects – investments they might have personal incentives to undertake. Second, tangible assets provide better collateral in borrowing than intangible assets.

The other leading model of financial policy, the *Pecking Order Theory*, argues that firms do not have well-defined target leverage ratios. According to this theory, asymmetric information and concomitant adverse selection problems lead managers to have a strict preference for internal over external financing and, when the firm must raise funds externally, for debt over equity financing. Observed capital structures are simply the result of past cash generated, investment requirements, and financing history. Consistent with the basic assumptions of this theory, the stock market reacts on average more negatively to the announcements of new equity issues than to debt issues. However, the evidence does not support its contention that equity financing is used only as a last resort after the firm's debt capacity has been exhausted. Many growth firms issue equity when their current leverage is below their debt capacity and thus the firm clearly could issue additional debt. Concerns about underinvestment and the costs of financial distress appear important in deciding on whether to raise funds through an equity offering – as the Tradeoff Theory suggests.

The negative reaction to new equity offerings presumably is driven by fears that corporate managers might attempt to sell overpriced shares to less-informed investors. Managers might mitigate this negative reaction if they could a convince investors that they are seeking equity to fund positive NPV projects, rather than simply timing the new issue to take advantage of perceived market mispricing. It is important to note that the negative market reactions to new equity issues are relatively small compared to the prior positive stock price increases that on average occur due to information releases about new investment opportunities. Ultimately, investment policy appears more important than financing policy in determining firm value.

While the evidence is inconsistent with the more extreme forms of the Pecking Order Theory, it is also not entirely consistent with the standard Tradeoff Theory. Growth firms often issue equity when the standard Tradeoff Theory suggests that they should issue more debt to move them back toward their leverage target. The *Strategic Financial Management* framework provides a potential explanation. In contrast to the standard Tradeoff Theory, which focuses on a single period, rational managers are likely to forecast future investment and financing requirements. Concerns about potential Underinvestment Problems can lead them to issue equity early in the process of undertaking a valuable new project, anticipating subsequent debt issues to complete the funding of the project and the conversion of this growth opportunity into a more tangible asset. Evidence from a large sample of Seasoned Equity Offerings (SEOs) reveals that the leverage of the typical equity issuer increases above its pre-SEO level over the following five years through the issuance of substantial amounts of new debt.

In summary, while no model or framework exists to inform managers exactly what capital structure to choose, the research provides useful guidance to managers for making leverage decisions. Financial managers appear to and probably should consider their firms' expected costs from financial distress and incentive-related agency issues – in particular, the Overinvestment and Underinvestment Problems – in making capital structure decisions. The firm's growth opportunities, asset tangibility, firm size, and regulatory status appear to be particularly important considerations (target leverage appears to decrease with growth opportunities and increase with firm size, regulation, and asset tangibility). Taxes, while not a primary determinant of capital structure for the typical firm, still may have some importance. Rational managers look beyond the current period, considering investment and financing requirements over their entire planning horizon and sequence their security issues accordingly.

9.3   Payout policy

Corporate payout policy addresses two basic questions: What is the appropriate size and form – dividends versus share repurchases – of distributions to shareholders? In the aggregate, firms distribute substantial amounts of cash to their shareholders; in recent years the cash paid to shareholders through both dividends and share repurchases has reached all-time highs. Although share repurchases were rare prior to the 1980s, they have exceeded dividend payments in many years following the mid-1990s.

The U.S. tax code has historically taxed capital gains at a lower rate than dividends for many, but not all, investors. Furthermore, the capital gains tax is not an accrual tax, investors can postpone this tax simply by delaying the sales of appreciated shares. Over the years, there has been a great deal of empirical research to determine whether taxes affect pre-tax expected stock returns (that is, the stock price). Results are quite mixed and fundamentally inconclusive. While it is difficult to draw definitive conclusions, it is relatively safe to say that there is no compelling evidence that differences in tax rates on dividends versus capital gains play a major role in affecting either corporate payout policies or stock prices. Also, empirical studies suggest that changes in the tax code do not appear to be the driving force behind the increased use of share repurchases over recent decades.

In contrast to demand-side considerations, such as those based on investor tax clienteles, the *Life-Cycle Theory* proposed by DeAngelo, DeAngelo and Stulz (2006) appears to explain the "broad brush features of observed payout policies." Younger growth firms often pay no cash to shareholders but retain it for investment purposes. The propensity to pay dividends is highest among larger, more profitable industrial companies and banks, which are noted for making particularly high and consistent dividend payouts. Mature firms often generate cash above that required to fund available positive NPV projects. Value maximization dictates that this cash be distributed to investors. Dividends and share repurchase provide methods to accomplish this.

It is reasonably well documented that most managers are reluctant to cut the firm's regular dividend. During recessionary periods, firms are more likely to cut share repurchases (or specially designated dividends, if they have been employed) than the firms' regular dividend. While dividends are discretionary relative to the interest payments on bonds, managers known reluctance to cut dividends helps to make dividend increases a reasonable commitment that the managers will continue to pay out future free cash flow – rather than waste it by investing in negative NPV projects.

Growth firms, with many valuable growth opportunities but little internally generated cash, even with no payouts, are likely to return to equity markets every three to five years in order to continue financing the exercise of their growth options. Value firms, with fewer growth opportunities but substantial amounts of internally generated cash, tend to have high payout rates – in fact, at rates high enough to force their return to external equity markets periodically, every eight to 12 years or so. Equity offerings are costly and lower cash payouts would allow value firms to make fewer of them. However, subjecting a firm to periodic due diligence investigations by sophisticated investment bankers can increase value – it helps to assure outside investors that managers are limiting investment to positive NPV projects.

Announcements of dividend changes tend to convey inside information to outside investors that causes significant changes in stock price. Dividend increases are generally greeted by positive stock returns, while decreases are met with negative market reactions. It is not entirely clear what the precise nature of this information might be, but recent evidence suggests that dividend changes (as well as changes in stock repurchases) are associated with future cash flow volatility. Why this information affects stock price is not entirely clear.

9.4 Concluding comments

Corporate finance is a pragmatically important and exciting topic (at least to us). While much progress has been made, there are still many unresolved questions and issues. At this point, we are faced with a problem that is like opening the box of a large jigsaw puzzle. The challenge is to arrange these pieces to form a coherent picture. Although you can study the individual pieces, it takes time and effort to arrange them in such a way that everything fits. And this task is even more challenging if some of the pieces are missing.

In some ways, we face a similar problem here. The academic community has documented evidence on an array of different facets related to explaining corporate financial decisions. But empirical research is ongoing. Today, some quite important pieces of evidence have yet to be explored. And just as the pieces of a jigsaw do not arrange themselves into a coherent picture, even a careful study of these individual pieces of evidence is not enough to produce a coherent theory of corporate financial policy. This creates valuable opportunities for future research: (1) Empirical research both on previously unexamined facets of financial policy decisions, as well as on re-examining other facets with greater precision, in addition to (2) theoretical research to find explanations that make more of this documented evidence fit together, thus providing a richer understanding of financial policy choices for both the academic and business communities. We expect that active research will continue in this area for years to come. It will be interesting to see what new insights are developed over the upcoming years.

Bibliography

Agrawal, Ankur, Emma Gibbs and Jean-Hugues Monier, 2015, *Building a Better Partnership between Finance and Strategy*, McKinsey & Company.

Akerlof, George A., 1970, The market for 'lemons': Quality uncertainty and the market mechanism, *The Quarterly Journal of Economics*, 84, 488–500.

Asquith, Paul and David W. Mullins, Jr., 1986, Equity issues and offering dilution, *Journal of Financial Economics*, 15, 61–89.

Baker, Malcolm and Jeffrey Wurgler, 2002, Market timing and capital structure, *The Journal of Finance*, 57, 1–32.

Barclay, Michael J. and Clifford W. Smith, 1988, Corporate payout policy: Cash dividends versus open-market repurchases, *Journal of Financial Economics*, 22, 61–82.

Barclay, Michael J. and Clifford W. Smith, 2005, The capital structure puzzle: The evidence revisited, *Journal of Applied Corporate Finance*, 17, 8–17.

Barclay, Michael J., Fangian Fu and Clifford W. Smith, 2021, Seasoned equity offerings and corporate financial management, *Journal of Corporate Finance*, 66.

Barclay, Michael J., Shane M. Heitzman and Clifford W. Smith, 2013, Debt and taxes: Evidence from the real estate industry, *Journal of Corporate Finance*, 20, 74–93.

Barclay, Michael J., Erwan Morellec and Clifford W. Smith, 2006, On the debt capacity of growth options, *The Journal of Business*, 79, 37–60.

Barclay, Michael J., Clifford W. Smith, and Ross L. Watts, 1995, The determinants of corporate leverage and dividend policies, *Journal of Applied Corporate Finance*, 7, 4–19.

Baxter, Nevins D., 1967, Leverage, risk of ruin and the cost of capital, *The Journal of Finance*, 22, 395–403.

Berk, Jonathan B. and Jules H. van Binsbergen, 2015, Measuring skill in the mutual fund industry, *Journal of Financial Economics*, 118, 1–20.

Bernoulli, Daniel, 1738, Specimen theoriae novae de mensura sortis, *Commentarii Academiae Scientiarum Imperialis Petropolitannae*.

Bertrand, Marianne and Antoinette Schoar, 2003, Managing with style: The effect of managers on firm policies, *The Quarterly Journal of Economics*, 118, 1169–1208.

Bhagat, Sanjai and Peter A. Frost, 1986, Issuing costs to existing shareholders in competitive and negotiated underwritten public utility equity offerings, *Journal of Financial Economics*, 15, 233–259.

Bhushan, Ravi, 1989, Firm characteristics and analyst following, *Journal of Accounting and Economics*, 11, 255–274.

Black, Fischer and Myron Scholes, 1973, The pricing of options and corporate liabilities, *Journal of Political Economy*, 81, 637–659.

Bradley, Michael, Gregg A. Jarrell and E. Han Kim, 1984, On the existence of an optimal capital structure: Theory and evidence, *The Journal of Finance*, 39, 857–878.

Brav, Alon, John R. Graham, Campbell R. Harvey and Roni Michaely, 2005, Payout policy in the 21st century, *Journal of Financial Economics*, 77, 483–527.

Brealey, Richard A, Stewart C. Myers and Franklin Allen, 2020 *Principles of Corporate Finance*, McGraw Hill.

Brennan, M. J., 1970, Taxes, market valuation and corporate financial policy, *National Tax Journal*, 23, 417–427.

Brickley, James A., 1983, Shareholder wealth, information signaling and the specially designated dividend: An Empirical Study, *Journal of Financial Economics*, 12, 187–209.

Brickley, James A., Clifford W. Smith and Jerold Zimmerman, 2021, *Managerial Economics and Organizational Architecture*, McGraw Hill.

Coase, Ronald H., 1937, The nature of the firm, *Economica*, 4, 386–405.

Coase, Ronald H., 1960, The problem of social cost, *Journal of Law and Economics*, 3, 1–44.

Comment, Robert and Gregg A. Jarrell, 1991, The relative signaling power of Dutch-auction and fixed-price self-tender offers and open-market share repurchases, *The Journal of Finance*, 46, 1243–1271.

Crutchley, Claire E. and Robert S. Hansen, 1989, A test of the agency theory of managerial ownership, corporate leverage, and corporate dividend, *Financial Management*, 18, 36–46.

Dann, Larry Y., 1981, Common stock repurchases, *Journal of Financial Economics*, 9, 113–138.

DeAngelo, Harry and Linda DeAngelo, 2006, The irrelevance of the MM dividend irrelevance theorem, *Journal of Financial Economics*, 79, 293–315.

DeAngelo, Harry, Linda DeAngelo and Douglas J. Skinner, 2004, Are dividends disappearing? Dividend concentration and the consolidation of earnings, *Journal of Financial Economics*, 72, 425–456.

DeAngelo, Harry, Linda DeAngelo and Douglas J. Skinner, 2007, Corporate payout policy, *Foundations and Trends in Finance*, 3, 95–287.

DeAngelo, Harry, Linda DeAngelo and Rene M. Stulz, 2006, Dividend policy and the earned/contributed capital mix: A test of the life-cycle theory, *Journal of Financial Economics*, 81, 227–254.

DeAngelo, Harry and Ronald W. Masulis, 1980, Optimal capital structure under corporate and personal taxation, *Journal of Financial Economics*, 8, 3–29.

DeAngelo, Linda Elizabeth, 1981, Auditor independence, 'low balling', and disclosure regulation, *Journal of Accounting and Economics*, 3, 113–127.

Denis, David J. and Igor Osobov, 2008, Why do firms pay dividends? International evidence on the determinants of dividend policy, *Journal of Financial Economics*, 89, 62–82.

Donaldson, Gordon, 1961, *Corporate Debt Capacity: A Study of Corporate Debt Policy and the Determinants of Corporate Debt Capacity*, Division of Research, Graduate School of Business Administration, Harvard University.

Dyl, Edward A. and Michael D. Joehnk, 1976, Competitive versus negotiated underwriting of public utility debt, *The Bell Journal of Economics*, 7, 680–689.

Easterbrook, Frank H., 1984, Two-agency cost explanations for dividends, *The American Economic Review*, 74, 650–659.

Eckbo, Espen B., 1986, Valuation effects of corporate debt, *Journal of Financial Economics*, 15, 119–151.

Ederington, Louis H., 1976, Negotiated versus competitive underwritings of corporate bonds, *The Journal of Finance*, 31, 17–28.

Fama, Eugene F., 1980, Agency problems and the theory of the firm, *Journal of Political Economy*, 88, 288–307.

Fama, Eugene F. and Kenneth R. French, 2015, A five-factor asset pricing model, *Journal of Financial Economics*, 116, 1–22.

Fama, Eugene F. and Michael C. Jensen, 1983, Separation of Ownership and Control, *Journal of Law and Economics*, 26, 301–325.

Fama, Eugene F. and Michael C. Jensen, 1985, Organizational forms and investment decisions, *Journal of Financial Economics*, 14, 101–119.

Fama, Eugene F. and Merton H. Miller, 1972, *The Theory of Finance*, Holt, Rinehart and Winston.

Fisher, Irving, 1930, *The Theory of Interest*, Macmillan.

Floyd, Eric, Nan Li and Douglas J. Skinner, 2015, Payout policy through the financial crisis: The growth of repurchases and the resilience of dividends, *Journal of Financial Economics*, 118, 299–316.

Frank, Murray Z. and Vidhan K. Goyal, 2008, Trade-off and pecking order theories of debt, *Handbook of Corporate Finance*, University of Minnesota, pp. 135–202.

Frank, Murray Z. and Vidhan K. Goyal, 2009, Capital structure decisions: Which factors are reliably important? *Financial Management*, 38, 1–37.

Fu Fangjian and Clifford W. Smith, 2021, Strategic financial management: Lessons from seasoned equity offerings, *Journal of Applied Corporate Finance*, 33, 22–35.

Graham, John R. and Campbell R. Harvey, 2001, The theory and practice of corporate finance: Evidence from the field, *Journal of Financial Economics*, 60, 187–243.

Graham, John R., Mark T. Leary and Michael R. Roberts, 2015, A century of capital structure: The leveraging of corporate America, *Journal of Financial Economics*, 118, 658–683.

Hansen, Robert S. and John M. Pinkerton, 1982, Direct equity financing: A resolution of a paradox, *The Journal of Finance*, 47, 651–665.

Harris, Milton and Artur Raviv, 1991, The theory of capital structure, *The Journal of Finance,* 46, 297–355.

Hermalin, Benjamin E. and Michael S. Weisbach, 2017, *The Handbook of the Economics of Corporate Governance*, Elsevier.

Jegadeesh, Narasimhan and Sheridan Titman, 1993, Returns to buying winners and selling losers: Implications for stock market efficiency, *The Journal of Finance*, 48, 65–91.

Jensen, Michael C., 1983, Organization theory and methodology, *The Accounting Review*, 58, 319–339.

Jensen, Michael C., 1986, Agency costs of free cash flow, corporate finance and takeovers, *The American Economic Review*, 76, 323–329.

Jensen, Michael C. and William H. Meckling, 1976, Theory of the firm: Managerial behavior, agency costs and ownership structure, *Journal of Financial Economics*, 3, 305–360.

Jung, Kooyul, Yong-Cheol Kim and Rene M. Stulz, 1996, Timing, investment opportunities, managerial discretion, and the security issue decision, *Journal of Financial Economics*, 42, 159–185.

Kalay, Avner and Michael Lemmon, 2008, Payout policy, *Handbook of Corporate Finance, Volume 2*, Elsevier, pp. 3–57.

Kalay, Avner and Adam Shimrat, 1987, Firm value and seasoned equity issues: Price pressure, wealth redistribution, or negative information, *Journal of Financial Economics*, 19, 109–126.

Kendall, Maurice, 1953, The analysis of economic time series: Part I: Prices, *Journal of the Royal Statistical Society*, 96, 11–25.

Kim, E. Han, John J. McConnell and Paul R. Greenwood, 1977, Capital structure rearrangements and me-first rules in an efficient capital market, *The Journal of Finance*, 32, 789–810.

Kothari, S. P., Thomas Lys, Clifford W.Smith, Ross L. Watts, Auditor liability and information disclosure, *Accounting Information and Management*, 3, 307–340.

Lemmon, Michael L, Michael R. Roberts and Jaime F. Zender, 2008, Back to the beginning: Persistence and the cross-section of corporate capital structure, *The Journal of Finance*, 63, 1575–1608.

Linn, Scott C. and Michael Pinegar, 1988, The effect of issuing preferred stock on common and preferred stockholder wealth, *Journal of Financial Economics*, 22, 155–184.

Lintner, John, 1956, Distribution of incomes of corporations among dividends, retained earnings and taxes, *The American Economic Review*, 46, 97–113.

Lintner, John, 1965, Security prices, risk, and maximal gains from diversification, *The Journal of Finance*, 20, 587–615.

Logue, Dennis E. and Robert A. Jarrow, 1978, Negotiation vs. competitive bidding in the sale of securities by public utilities, *Financial Management*, 7, 31–39.

Long, Michael S. and Ileen B. Malitz, 1985, The investment financing nexus: Some empirical evidence, *Midland Corporate Finance Journal*, 4, 53–59.

Mandelbrot, Benoit, 1966, Forecasts of future prices, unbiased markets, and martingale models, *Journal of Business*, 39, 242–255.

Markowitz, Harry, 1952, Portfolio selection, *The Journal of Finance*, 7, 77–91.

Masulis, Ronald W. and Ashok N. Korwar, 1986, Seasoned equity offerings: An empirical investigation, *Journal of Financial Economics*, 15, 91–118.

Mayers, David and Clifford W. Smith, 1982, On the corporate demand for insurance, *Journal of Business*, 55, 281–296.

McConnell John J. and Chris J. Muscarella, 1985, Corporate capital expenditure decisions and the market value of the firm, *Journal of Financial Economics*, 14, 399–422.

Merton, Robert C., 1973, Theory of rational option pricing, *The Bell Journal of Economics*, 4, 141–183.

Merton, Robert C., 1974, On the pricing of corporate debt: The risk structure of interest rates, *The Journal of Finance*, 29, 449–470.

Michaely, Roni, Stefano Rossi and Michael Weber, 2021, Signaling safety, *Journal of Financial Economics*, 139, 405–427.

Miller, Merton H., 1977, Debt and taxes, *The Journal of Finance*, 32, 261–275.

Miller, Merton H. and Franco Modigliani, 1961, Dividend policy, growth, and the valuation of shares, *The Journal of Business*, 34, 411–433.

Modigliani, Franco and Merton H. Miller, 1958, The cost of capital, corporation finance and the theory of investment, *The American Economic Review*, 48, 261–297.

Modigliani, Franco and Merton H. Miller, 1963, Corporate income taxes and the cost of capital: A correction, *The American Economic Review*, 53, 433–443.

Murphy, Kevin J., 1985, Corporate performance and managerial remuneration: An empirical analysis, *Journal of Accounting and Economics*, 7, 11–42.

Myers, Stewart C., 1977, Determinants of corporate borrowing, *Journal of Financial Economics*, 5, 147–175.

Myers, Stewart C., 1984, The capital structure puzzle, *The Journal of Finance*, 39, 575–592.

Myers, Stewart C. and Nicholas S. Majluf, 1984, Corporate financing and investment decisions when firms have information that investors do not have, *Journal of Financial Economics*, 13, 187–221.

Nyatee, Anisha, 2021, Asset redeployability and capital structure choice: The role of competition, *International Journal of Economics, Commerce and Management*, 9, 337–387.

Osborne, M. F. M., 1959, Brownian motion in the stock market, *Operations Research*, 7, 145–273.

Osborne, M. F. M, 1962, Periodic structure in the Brownian motion of stock prices, *Operations Research*, 10, 285–420.

Ovtchinnikov, Alexei V., 2010, Capital structure decisions: Evidence from deregulated industries, *Journal of Financial Economics*, 95, 249–274.

Oztekin, Ozde, 2015, Capital structure decisions around the world: Which factors are reliably important? *Journal of Financial and Quantitative Analysis*, 50, 301–323.

Porter, Michael E., 2008, *Competitive Strategy*, Free Press.

Rajan, Raghuram G. and Luigi Zingales, 1995, What do we know about capital structure? Some evidence from international data, *The Journal of Finance*, 50, 1421–1460.

Roll, Richard, 1994, What every CFO should know about scientific progress in financial economics: What is known and what remains to be resolved, *Financial Management*, 23, 69–75.

Ross, Stephen A., 1977, The determination of financial structure: The incentive-signaling approach, *The Bell Journal of Economics*, 8, 23–40.

Rozeff, Michael S., 1982, Growth, beta, and agency costs as determinants of dividend payout ratios, *The Journal of Financial Research*, 5, 249–259.

Rubinstein, Mark, 2002, Markowitz's 'Portfolio Selection': A fifty-year retrospective, *The Journal of Finance*, 57, 1041–1045.

Samuelson, Paul, 1965, Proof that properly anticipated prices fluctuate randomly, *Industrial Management Review*, 6, 41–49.

Scholes, Myron S., 1972, The market for securities: Substitution versus price pressure and the effects of information on share prices, *Journal of Business*, 45, 179–211.

Seyhun, H. Nejat, 1986, Insider's profits, costs of trading, and market efficiency, *Journal of Financial Economics*,16, 189–212.

Shanken, Jay and Clifford W. Smith, 1996, Implications of capital market research for corporate finance, *Financial Management*, 25, 98–104.

Sharpe, William F., 1964, Capital asset prices: A theory of market equilibrium under conditions of risk, *The Journal of Finance*, 19, 425–442.

Smith, Clifford W., 1976, Option Pricing, *Journal of Financial Economics*, 3, 3–5.

Smith, Clifford W., 1977, Alternative methods for raising capital: Rights versus underwritten offerings, *Journal of Financial Economics*, 5, 273–307.

Smith, Clifford W., 1979, Applications of option pricing analysis, *Handbook of Financial Economics*, North-Holland/Elsevier, pp. 80–121.

Smith, Clifford W., 1986a, Investment banking and the capital acquisition process, *Journal of Financial Economics*, 15, 3–29.

Smith, Clifford W., 1986b, Raising capital: Theory and evidence, *Midland Corporate Financial Journal*, 4, 6–22.

Smith, Clifford W., 1990, The theory of corporate finance: A historical overview, *The Modern Theory of Corporate Finance*, McGraw Hill, pp. 3–24.

Smith, Clifford, W., 1991, Globalization of financial markets, *Carnegie-Rochester Conference Volume on Public Policy (Spring)*, 77–96.

Smith, Clifford W. and Jerold B. Warner, 1979, On financial contracting: An analysis of bond covenants, *Journal of Financial Economics*, 117–161.

Smith, Clifford W. and Ross L. Watts, 1982, Incentive and tax effects of executive compensation plans, *Australian Journal of Manage*ment, 7, 139–157.

Smith, Clifford W. and Ross L. Watts, 1992, The investment opportunity set and corporate financing, dividend and compensation policies, *Journal of Financial Economics*, 32, 263–292.

Spence, A. Michael, 1973, Time and communication in economic and social interaction, *The Quarterly Journal of Economics*, 87, 651–660.

Stanley, David T. and Marjorie L. Girth, 1971, *Bankruptcy: Problem, Process and Reform*, Brookings Institution.

Taggart, Robert A., Jr., 1977, A model of corporate financing decisions, *The Journal of Finance*, 32, 1467–1484.

Titman, Sheridan and Sergey Tsyplakov, 2007, A dynamic model of optimal capital structure, *Review of Finance*, 11, 401–451.

Titman, Sheridan and Roberto Wessels, 1988, The determinants of capital structure choice, *The Journal of Finance*, 43, 1–19.

Treynor, Jack, 1962, Toward a theory of market value of risky assets, unpublished manuscript.

Van Horne, James C., 1974, Corporate liquidity and bankruptcy, working paper, Stanford University.

Wakeman, L. Macdonald, 1998, The real function of bond rating agencies, *The Revolution in Corporate Finance, 3rd edn.*, Blackwell Publishers, pp. 25–28.

Warner, Jerold B., 1977, Bankruptcy costs: Some evidence, *The Journal of Finance*, 32, 337–347.

Working, Holbrook, 1934, A random-difference series for use in the analysis of time series, *Journal of the American Statistical Association*, 29, 11–24.

Zeng, Liyu and Priscilla Luk, 2020, Examining share repurchasing and the S&P buyback indices in the U.S. market, S&P Dow Jones indices. https://www .spglobal.com/spdji/en/documents/research/research-sp-examining-share -repurchases-and-the-sp-buyback-indices.pdf

Zingales, Luigi, 1998, Survival of the fittest or the fattest? Exit and financing in the trucking industry, *The Journal of Finance*, 53, 905–938.

Index